Hard IS Only Half THE Story

REAL ADVENTURES FROM MY JOURNEY INTO THE UNKNOWN

WRITTEN BY

Wendy Zahorjanski

ILLUSTRATED BY MIRJAM KLOP

On the internet:
www.wendyzahorjanski.com

Contact the author:
info@wendyzahorjanski.com

To my fellow Cross-Cultural Workers.

Trekking the unknown is not for the faint of heart.

May each brave step lead you into deeper fellowship with Jesus. It's my hope that this book will encourage you to keep following the voice of the Guide and inspire you to look for the treasures hidden along the way, no matter how deep the shadows grow.

TABLE OF CONTENTS

EXPLORING THE WOODS

A voice whispers, "just follow the path"
I'm not afraid at first.
But as I walk it, the branches twist
And in shadows I become immersed.

Everything glows a different hue
Under their shadowy haze.
Small and alone I walk along
Overwhelmed: in a daze.

The shadows deepen, my feet start running
I don't see it sticking out.
A root put there on purpose I'm sure
I trip and fall: blackout.

When I return to consciousness
My body's all bruises and aches.
Every fiber of my being is seething
I'm hurt for goodness sake.

"Where's the adventure?" I'm screaming now
"You promised it before.
I listened and I trusted you
But now I'm lost and sore".

So there I sit in silence
The woods have finally won.
My emotions drained, my willpower gone
I stare ahead. I'm numb.

It's in the quiet that she comes,
Slowly, as if unsure.
When she sees me, she stops and stares
And I stare back at her.

The most beautiful brown to match the leaves
She's gleaming in the sun.
The light is shining, I hadn't noticed
I was too busy coming undone.

Her eyes are kind, is that even possible?
It's like she knows my name.
She turns and walks away from me
I stand up, forgetting my pain.

It's just a deer, but not to me
She's a jewel of the woods.
A breath of life, a shift in sight
She's everything that's good.

A longing comes to follow her,
Along her path. Wait, what?
A trail, oh wow I see it now.
I'm not as lost as I thought.

And more than that, the wood's transformed
And my fear has melted away.
Something new has grasped my heart,
A wonder words can't convey.

"Yes, there's wonder in the hard,"
Says a voice now familiar to me.
"Now follow close, I know the way.
I'll lead you through these trees."

Chapter 1:

EXPOSED

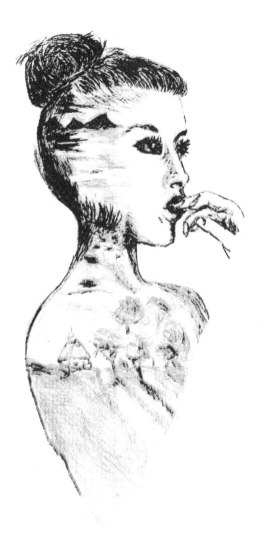

A voice whispers, "just follow the path"
I'm not afraid at first.

It's the same dream again. I rush to get ready. The alarm is mysteriously silent. The same thought goes through my mind. *I can't be late. Hurry up.* The look on people's faces when I arrive. *Why are they all staring like that?* The horror as I look down at myself, trying to see what is obvious to everyone else. I am naked, completely and utterly naked.

The camera pulls back. The view is aerial now as if even my dream knows that I need extra help: help to find a place to hide, to cover up and stop the eyes from searing my exposed skin. Time stands still. Terrified, I frantically search for escape. There are no dark corners or green bushes in this cruel dream and even if there were, my feet are cement. I can't move. I just stand there in my birthday suit. Unfortunately, there is no cake. There aren't any balloons: one would surely have been enough if held just right, but I have no such luck.

Other than my lack of clothes, everything in the scene is normal. A group of friends stand off to the side talking. As more people enter the room, some walk with purpose. Others don't. I am the only thing that doesn't fit: I am the only one who forgot her clothes. Then, I wake up. The dream is over.

The book in front of you is my nakedness on display. My bare thoughts and experiences exposed for all to see. I am willing to open my inner world to you, but only under one condition, I ask that my honest effort be met with kindness. Be sharp, be vigilant, discern well, but allow kindness to fill in the cracks.

This book is my attempt to faithfully retell all that I have lived, but perfection is not to be found in these pages. Adjust your expectations accordingly. My story is filled with mess-ups. I've fallen only to get up again, to fall again, to get up again, but that is the cycle of learning. I invite you to come alongside me. I am honored that out of all the stories you could have invested your precious time in, you've chosen mine.

Thank you for giving me a chance amidst the information-soaked world we live in. I do not take my task lightly and as I am peeled back layer by layer before you, I hope that your courage is ignited in order that you too might enter into the unknown, whatever that may mean for your story.

That reoccurring dream, which I actually do have, was the last thing on my mind as I looked out the airplane window. If I had known how much the next decade of my life would typify that dream, how raw life would leave me feeling, I wouldn't have been so content in my daydream at thirty thousand feet.

Ticket Stub—
Bishkek Here I
Come!

The beginning of
the Journey...

Chapter 2:

NO-MAN'S-LAND

But as I walk it, the branches twist
And in shadows I become immersed.

"Just get a one-month visa when you get off the plane at the airport," I was assured over the phone before packing my bags for what would prove to be the beginning of my international living. "We will be there to pick you up."

"Ok, I've got this. No big deal. Sounds simple enough," I reassured myself as I packed my bag and an extra bag for my brother, the mastermind of this whole operation. After weighing, shifting, packing, repacking, and slimming down, I was ready.

I had one huge duffle bag, one big blue plastic tub and a backpack, all packed to the weight limit by the gram. My adrenaline surged at the prospect of adventure and new things. Back home, my audience lacked my enthusiasm as I shared about my plan to drop out of college, quit my job and move to, "Where was it again? K something?" At the time, it felt like a lot them thought I was crazy.

The questions came and almost always were accompanied with that look of, 'I'm not so sure', but I didn't care. I just wanted out. Out of my life; out of my country. This seemed like the ideal out, a fluorescent 'Exit' sign, my knight in shining armor.

Exiting is a required first step before entering something new. There must be an exit, a leaving, a stepping-out-of in order for there to be a stepping-into. This is a type of goodbye to what was because changes are coming. And while the goodbye part was not a struggle for me, the entering into a new thing proved much more difficult.

For some, leaving is the greatest sacrifice. It's the step that cuts and strips down, but I had a deep calm about my choice to move halfway around the world with no specific plan or time frame. Some people call that 'knowing in your gut' but I think it was even deeper than my gut. It was a soul-calm, if you will.

Nothing about my life at that time was calm, so any kind of peace was noticeable. I felt lost and directionless, like most nineteen-year-olds do. So, departing from my familiar life to jump into the unknown didn't sound all that bad.

I was going to miss my family; the half that I was leaving, my mom, sister, brother-in-law and their four children (the fifth came along after I moved). But, on the other side of the world, my brother, sister-in-law and their two children would be waiting for me when I landed. I knew they would introduce me to their home and community. I have no doubt that this helped lighten the goodbye knowing that family would be waiting for me.

I said goodbye to my mom, the woman who modeled for me and taught me that the Lord is the same no matter the location, a lesson that I still draw on today. Her love for and trust in the Lord laid a solid foundation for my life. It also freed her to release me to live out my call far from her: an act of the deepest trust. I will be forever grateful that her trust allowed her to see me off with full support amidst the tears. A gift I keep receiving from her.

I also said goodbye to being the aunt that my nieces and nephew would be making face-to-face memories with and to being a sister who could pop over any time for a cup of coffee or to watch a show. This sacrifice was felt over time and not necessarily in the initial goodbye. In that moment, my urge to go pushed the sacrifice down into the recesses of my heart.

It would take years for it to come back to the surface, to be felt and then laid before the One who knows the sacrifice of goodbye. At that point, I was held by the wonder of what this new place would hold for me and nothing else.

THE INSANE RUSH

"Why not move here and figure it out?" my brother said as if he was suggesting I have a side salad instead of French fries with my dinner and not that I uproot my entire life.

"Why not?" was my response only because I couldn't think of any reason not to move and figure it out. *What do I have to lose?* I thought. *A job I don't like and school I can't pay for.* My boyfriend had just broken up with me, so that was already lost. All in all, not an impressive list.

"Ok, I'll go," I said.

I had no idea that one simple decision, driven by a desire for change, would be the beginning of my 'goings'. It was the first step of moving out of what I knew and into something completely foreign.

As the stories contained in these pages unfold, you will see that with each challenge I am called to a deeper level of trust in my Guide. I must embrace greater openness to change; change around me and change in me. That is the hard part. Had I known all that it meant to move across the globe, learn a new language, make friends from a different culture, and worship in a different style, I would have thought twice about going. And there are the endless ways each of those things would leave me feeling helpless and incompetent (a fancy word for dumb). I did not know any of them. Often, grace is hidden in not knowing everything.

It did not take long for 'different' to startle me; that happened as soon as the plane touched down in hot, dusty Bishkek. I am not exaggerating by saying that the nanosecond the wheels touched that runway, every person jumped to their feet and reached up to retrieve their carry-ons from the overhead bin. Every person except me.

The seat belt sign was still on. The plane was still moving. I had never seen anything like this in my life and in that moment, I was convinced that there was exactly one sane human on the plane and that person was the only one still sitting. No one could move until the plane taxied to the gate and the door opened anyway, so why rush? Also, the pushing seemed extreme. I was not about to push my way through the aisle and into a terminal I had never seen in order to get a visa I had no idea where to get. So, I just sat and waited: a mistake I would soon regret.

I stepped off the plane and followed the mob in front of me, at a safe distance, eyes scanning for that magical sign that read 'Visas, Get Your Visas Here'. I had to get my visa before going through passport control because of the international world's love of stickers. My scanning was a matter of survival. "I've got this," I whispered to myself. I was not a novice traveler and airports didn't intimidate me, but this was my first international solo travel experience and when every sign is written with letters that your brain cannot place any meaning to, panic inevitably creeps in.

If I can't find that visa sign, will I become like Tom Hanks's character and live in this terminal indefinitely? The scene flashed through my mind. There I was, sleeping on the chairs, collecting and returning carts for loose change to buy a burger, which was all ridiculous because there were no chairs, no carts, and no fast food stands. I was caught in no-man's-land.

No-man's-land is not a place where life happens. It's more like a hallway meant to be walked through without stopping. Thanks to my lack of experience and understanding, my feet came to a halt right in the middle of that 'hallway.'

No one stopped to help me. No one asked if I was lost. I know I definitely looked lost. Half of the passengers were already through customs, still pushing and rushing, slowly fading out of sight. *Maybe there is a time limit on how long I can be in no-man's-land: stranded between plane and city.* Panic was soon joined by isolation. *There it is!* I smiled as I saw that wonderful word—Visa—written in letters that my brain could compute.

I went up to the window and a form was shoved under the glass, no smile, no explanation. This scene has become familiar to me over the years. Going to get paperwork done will involve at least one smileless face and several forms that do not make sense and are not explained. But then, I was still in no-man's-land: nothing was familiar.

Thankfully, this was a simple form only requiring basic information about me along with my signature. I knew all the answers. With my new shiny sticker in my passport—my ticket out of the in-between —I went through passport control: last.

THE FINAL HURDLE

I was the last person in that section of the airport and it felt creepy. If there had been anyone left, I would have pushed my way past them, just so I wouldn't be left behind. Suddenly, pushing didn't seem so unreasonable. I was delusional and jet-lagged. Since there was no one around to push my way past and prove my incredibly accurate grasp of the culture, I just walked through, trying to figure out where baggage claim was hiding.

This was not a problem, since I was stuck in the hallway that funnels toward the outside world and baggage claim was the last stop before freedom. Finding my bags was not a problem either because they were the only ones sitting on the carousel.

I took a deep breath, remembering my shiny, new sticker in my passport. I was doing it and it felt good. All I needed was a cart and I could walk out those doors to my new life and waiting sister-in-law. My eyes started scanning once again.

This time it would be easy, no letters just a shape; a familiar shape. *The carts can't look that different here. Where are they?* There weren't any. I looked everywhere and there was not a single cart to be found. All of the sudden my mind flashed back to the mad dash at touchdown. They were not afraid of being the last one in no-man's-land, they just wanted a cart!

I could lift the 50-pound duffle bag, barely, but the 50-pound tub, no way. Oh, and together, 100% no way. *Why is there not one single person to help me? Why wasn't I warned about the cart shortage? What else was I not warned about? What else is waiting for me on the other side of those doors?* Panic increased the number and speed of my thoughts as it was joined by its pal, trepidation. Slowly this was becoming an extension of the no-man's-land I thought I had just escaped.

After several failed attempts at heavy-luggage juggling, I figured out that if I stacked the duffle bag on the tub I could slowly push them across the tile floor. The only minor problem was that I couldn't see where I was going as I bent over and pushed.

I had to stop every few feet to look up and reorient myself. Push, push, stop, look up, reorient. Push, push, stop, look up, reorient. This was not how I envisioned crossing the threshold into my new home. It did not look pretty and I was not having a good time. The doors opened and I push-pushed my way through. I was instantly hit with the dry heat as the sun shone through big glass windows. My ears were bombarded by taxi drivers fighting for business, "Taxi! Taxi! You need taxi?" Each one was pushing a precious cart.

I narrowed my eyes and stared them all down. "No, I don't."

I had stopped just outside the doors of baggage claim to wait for my ride to see me. There were so many taxi drivers blocking my way that I was sure she would see me before I saw her. Stopping was my second mistake. As soon as I stood up to reorient myself and look around, a taxi driver swooped in and started putting my bags on his cart.

"I give you ride. What is your address?"

I was stunned. "I don't need a taxi! No—stop." I removed my bags from that coveted cart and on I pushed.

Each taxi driver was just as pushy and I had to fight them off one by one.

Where is my ride? I'm sure that I stick out like a sore thumb, so why can't she see me? I couldn't see her either.

Another taxi driver with another cart approached.

"No," I said, too loudly. I had almost screamed at him before he got close enough to offer his service. I was overwhelmed and sweaty and I had no ride. I wanted to turn around and go right back where I came from, but I didn't know how.

"Do you need a taxi? If not, can I practice my English with you while you wait for your ride?" He asked.

"What?" I blurted out.

"Can I practice my English by talking with you while you wait for your ride? You can put your bags on my cart while we wait. We can sit on that bench right there by the doors so we can watch for your ride," he said.

I kept waiting for the catch, but it never came. He was just being kind. He put my bags on his cart and we sat and talked for an hour or so. I have no idea what we talked about. Maybe family, food, and hobbies: universal topics. As other passengers came through those doors arriving on flights after mine, I watched as each got bombarded by the taxi drivers. Head held high and eyes fixed straight ahead they just pushed their way through; just a typical Tuesday.

With each "taxi" yelled, I was more thankful for my buffer, my taxi driver who would ironically never drive me in his taxi. He was the closest thing I had at that airport to a friend.

REASSURED AMIDST UNCERTAINTY

Now I see that it was not the power of his presence alone that drove away my loneliness and insecurity, but the reminder that he was of the faithful Presence that always goes with me. It was this Presence that was familiar to me and brought comfort. He had sent the bodily presence of the taxi driver, to remind me that I was never alone.

Somehow, that simple reminder set my mind above the moment and its accompanying emotions. It breathed the familiar into a completely foreign setting, something I would experience over and over again. I was still overwhelmed and sweaty, but my spirit was comforted. I was helpless and did not understand most of the words that were being spoken around me, but kindness had broken through all of the chaos and in rushed peace.

This doesn't mean that, when my sister-in-law flew through the door, I didn't breathe a huge sigh of relief. I did. It also doesn't mean that fear was absent. The thought, *what if no one comes?*, was playing in my mind on repeat. But through that man's kind act, I felt remembered. Feeling remembered, especially by the Presence, is powerful. That Presence is the fullness of peace and hope and knowledge, all especially lacking when one is surrounded by a strange and unknown world.

My ride had come, and with it my invitation to take a step deeper into the chaos that I had just tasted. She apologized several times for being late and thanked the taxi driver several times for keeping me company. He walked with us out to the car, pushing the cart loaded with my bags. He would not take money, even when we insisted, and so with one more "thank you" we left him in the parking lot and drove into the city towards my new everything.

GREAT THINGS?

If someone had asked me about my expectations for moving overseas, I probably would have replied with an adapted William Carey quote. I was expecting great things from God and planning to attempt great things for God. Emphasis on my attempting, which to me meant accomplishing.[1]

I had no doubt in my mind that I wanted to do great things for God. Because of that, I was willing to go anywhere and do anything. But I didn't understand that 'great things' come on a spectrum: often with me on one end and the Lord on the other.

This difference in perspective would lead to disappointment and discouragement on my part. 'Great things' to me were revivals, culture being shifted because of the infusion of the gospel, new Bible translations. No doubt these are great and awesome things, but now, I believe that the Lord looks more to the 'great things' of a person's inner world.

I believe that my desire and willingness to go was for Him great, even though the desire was actually the work of His own Spirit in me; it was a desire that started in His heart and was transplanted into mine. My absorbing of His desire brings Him pleasure even if it will take a lifetime for that desire to be refined and tweaked and, even if this vision is not perfectly executed in the present life, the desire is enough for Him.

He revels in working on the heart level, from which desires spring. It's when the heart is hard and there is no desire that

[1] William Carey, "The Missionary Herald" The Baptist Magazine, Volume 35, January 1843.

He cannot work. An over-zealous or naïve desire is no problem. He knows that we are children and often do not fully understand the why behind what we desire and so He does the most incredible thing. He gives Himself entirely to us, promising to remain with us throughout the entire process. I often miss the weight of this.

No matter where I am in the process, the excitement of the beginning, the lostness of the in-between, the disappointment of unrealized hopes, the shame of desires twisted, or even the joy of harvest, He is right beside me. He is right beside us, loving, redirecting, purifying, delighting in you and me: His children.

The process of living life is apt to beat these truths out of us if we do not guard our hearts and minds. Resist the lie that we have to have everything all figured out. We don't and that is fine with Him.

Roll that burden of the unknown onto Him, who holds all knowledge and wisdom, only He is worthy to carry it. Then you will be ready to go for it: whatever desire He has grafted into your heart. Living the process will change you, but I think if you are honest you would admit that parts of you are desperate for change. I know that parts of me are.

THE NEW PLACE

The next several months in this new place would be the beginning of that long process of redefining and tweaking in me. It felt like an endless hallway instead of an entering into a new life. It wasn't terrible. The people I met, most of them at least, remain precious to me. The language I started to learn, fascinating. I can still smell the city and feel the careening of the *Marshutka* (the city bus) flying through the streets. I loved it, but I felt lost, stuck in the in-between, neither here nor there. Can you relate?

Have you tried something new? I was trying to learn the bus system in a city of 800,000 people. My hometown in Vermont has a little over 2,000. The contrast was staggering.

Are you ready? Do you have energy? Are you open to learn? Good. You're going on a trip.

You hop on the bus, which is actually a 15-passenger van with some of the seats taken out. You're off.

You have committed to stick with the new experience to the end and are confident that you will succeed. Everything is different than you are used to, but you roll with it.

The bus/van turns. No problem. You already know that you have to have the turns memorized because seeing out the windows is impossible due to the number of people crammed inside.

You are doing well, picking up new things, adapting, learning and then, all of a sudden, the bus/van turns again.

Wait, that was supposed to be a right turn. Did we turn right? Maybe it just felt like we went left. Wow, it's hot in here. I'll just ask. You look up into the armpit of the man next to you. *What's the word for right? Levo? Or is it pravo? I can't remember which is which. I'll just say the one I think.* Another jerk to the right. *Never mind, that turn was definitely a right turn and I am definitely lost. Ok, what do I do now? Get off the bus? I have no idea where I am.*

You decide to ride on, trying to figure out what to do. Slowly the people call the bus/van to stop and hop off. There are no designated bus stops, you just yell out, "stop!" when you want to get off and the driver pulls slightly off the road so you can jump out. "Stop!" you want to yell, but fear causes a pause and the armpit takes advantage. He beats you to it and hops off. The bus/van is moving again before you manage to push your way to the door.

"Stop!" calls one. "Stop!" another.

The bus is now empty and the driver pulls off the road. You still wait, holding on to a lost hope that all those right turns had magically equaled the left you needed and you would recognize your surroundings. You do not.

The driver turns around and says something to you. You strain to listen, your brain computing. Language lessons pay off. You understand. It is the end of the bus line. It goes no further, so you hop off acting like that is just where you wanted to be and for the first time in half an hour you can see the world outside.

You turn to the left, then the right. The bus drives away. Nothing is familiar and even worse: the city has somehow disappeared behind you. All those rights took you right out of town. You are lost, really lost.

Panic and loneliness creep in. *Why did I try something new? Will I ever feel like I belong? Will all the differences ever make sense? Is there even a purpose for them, other than to confuse me?*

The tears well up. It is all a bit too much. The enthusiasm is gone and you just want to go home, back to where things make sense. You pull out your cell phone and call your big brother. Embarrassed, but glad to hear his voice, you ask him to come pick you up. He rushes to do just that and his familiar face is almost as beautiful as the snow-covered mountains you might have ended up in if the bus line did not stop where it did.

He is glad to see you and sorry that you got so lost. He doesn't even tease you. He knows what it's like to try something new and get hopelessly lost because of it. You can see the understanding in his eyes. Kindness. For a moment you are set above the chaos and at peace. Then you head back into the city. Tomorrow you will try again.

CLOSE, NOT PERFECT

I got lost too many times to count. I missed appointments, language lessons, and hang-out times with friends. I came home crying, believing that I couldn't do it. I never did learn the bus/van system perfectly, but I got better. It became less daunting to squeeze onto the van and at times I actually caught myself enjoying the ride.

Sometimes, I got lost so close to my destination that I could call a friend to walk me through the remainder of my journey. Other times I had to rely on my big brother. This rubbed against my independent, self-reliant western self. This is a rubbing that continues until this day, even though I am now being rubbed by a different source. Slowly though, the unpleasant rubbing is changing me.

Letting go of things that I previously considered part of my personality creates significant internal friction. I had always been proud of my independence and self-reliance, considering it a part of who I was. But getting lost so many times and walking down that long hallway of the in-between has opened a new world to me: a world of inter-dependence and God-reliance.

I now see my foolishness. What I once thought was an essential part of me was a crooked part. A part warped by the sin inside me and a culture around me. I see now that I can live without it, better yet that it can be remade, straightened by a Skilled Hand. If I had not braved no-man's-land, the crookedness would have remained. The hallway does lead somewhere and walking along it brought me to an amazing realization. The unknown is actually an invitation to enrichment. That invitation, when understood, is hard to refuse.

Things Worth Remembering

- *Exiting is simple: entering is a process*
- *Being in unfamiliar surroundings is overwhelming*
- *Kindness can birth peace amidst chaos*
- *Human kindness is just a taste of the kindness of God*
- *Try new things!*
- *The hallway leads somewhere*

My brother and I

The mountains I almost ended
up on during my epic bus ride

Chapter 3:

SLOWING DOWN TO SEE

The shadows deepen, my feet
start running
I don't see it sticking out.

I had walked the hallway and some of the daze had worn off. I knew exactly where I was as I stood waiting for the light to turn green. Finally, I knew where I was going and I even knew how to get there. And as an unexpected bonus, I was talking on the phone with a friend, which meant that I *had* a friend.

As I slowly settled into life, some of the strange things were becoming not so strange. I was not talking to my friend about anything important, we were just chatting. All of the sudden, as the light was changing from red to green the man next to me grabbed my arm; tightly grabbed my arm. Had he been big, I might have been unnerved, but as I glanced sideways, I saw someone small with many years behind him, so I just tried to shake him off. His grip tightened. *Surely he will let go of my arm as I start to cross the street*, I thought. I gave one last shake and stepped out into the road. He was right beside me, grip tightening again.

We were crossing multiple lanes of traffic in front of cars waiting impatiently for their light to turn green. I knew I had to be on the other side by the time that light changed because their daily capacity available for waiting had been exhausted by the long lines at the post office, leaving nothing left for traffic lights. The moment that light blinked green they would hit the gas.

"This guy won't let go of my arm," I told my friend in English. "He's probably drunk. Ugggh, how annoying. When I get to the other side I can't wait to tell him how rude he is being...Huh, I don't remember the road being this wide."

I picked up my pace. The stranger picked up his. He was not pulling me toward himself, but matching his steps to mine. I sped up again with a shake of my arm. He tightened his grip again and sped up with me. Stepping onto the sidewalk on the other side of the street, I told my friend a quick "bye" and turned toward the man to give him a piece of my mind. Before I could open my mouth, he released his grip and started to walk away. I thought I heard him mutter "Thank you" under his breath.

I stood staring at his back as he walked slowly away, sweeping his cane back and forth as he went. My eyes widened. I wanted to run up to him and tell him I was so sorry. I looked back at the road behind me, cars whizzing by and then back at his slow, methodical steps. I closed my eyes and then heard a familiar Voice.

"Sometimes, you are so distracted that you don't see what I have put right in front of you." It spoke to my heart.

I looked down at my phone, still in my right hand. If only I had just taken a moment to look at the man before we crossed the road, but I hadn't. Men don't usually grab my arm, so I should have known that something extraordinary was happening.

He was almost out of sight now, carefully following the strip of tactile paving on the sidewalk made to guide those with eyes that could not. I had been trying to leave a vision impaired person in the middle of a busy intersection. In my distraction, I had not noticed that the man beside me, who I was determined to shake off was hanging on for dear life. He said thank you because I had helped him to cross the street. He had walked right next to me across four lanes of traffic and I had not even looked over at him with enough interest to notice that he needed my help.

THE LESSON

How many other 'blind men' have I not noticed? I don't know, but I am sure there are others. It is important here to pause and say that I did not feel condemned by that Voice.

That Voice did not say, "Idiot, how did you not notice he needed assistance?" That was my own inner critic.

This Voice was different. What it said made me sad, but in the sense that I had missed out on something. If I had realized that the man needed help, I would have hung up right away and helped him across the road, giving him my full attention. I love helping people. I don't mind going out of my way to do so.

There have been several times that I have carried heavy grocery bags for the elderly as we walked along the same road, chatting. I have even sent Danny back to find an old man whose grocery bag had ripped, spilling bottles of cooking oil onto the pavement in front of him. I had been carrying too many groceries myself to be of use, but texted Danny to bring a bag and come help. Danny did, and not only that, but visited this man many times and carried many more groceries for him.

It was not that I was unwilling to help. It was that I did not even realize that help was required. The need was right in front of my face, but I was too engulfed in my own world to see it. I was not even doing something important, but this problem plagues me as I spend a significant amount of each day distracted.

It might not seem like a big deal, talking on the phone while waiting at a traffic light and it isn't. What I was doing was not wrong. By itself that choice was not harmful, but became so as it made me oblivious to what was going on around me. It stole my energy and attention away from the thing that really needed focus.

Can I confess something to you? I am terrible at living in the moment. I am all about efficiency. If I can take care of a phone call as I walk to the store, that is efficient. If I can answer a few texts as I play with my son without him noticing, that is efficient. If I can fill every moment of every day with productivity, that is my dream come true. There is just one problem. Jesus, who is the ultimate example of what is good and right and wise, was not solely focused on efficiency.

In some ways, my desire to be efficient does reflect the heart of God. He created us to make things, to work, to produce. Our incredible minds, also His gift, come up with brilliant ways to decrease the effort and expense needed to accomplish things. This amazes me.

We have been given incredible resources and I think it is wise to examine how they can be used with the least effort possible. The danger is that we do not know when to stop. I fear it has become an obsession to do more with less, faster. Production has become the ultimate goal. The more you produce, the more you are valued. But this endlessly busy way of life has nothing to do with the life that Jesus lived.

Not all efficiency is rooted in acquiring or producing more material things either. Most of us who are trying to emulate the example left by Jesus recognize that the accumulation of money, accolades or stuff, is not the goal. We are much more subtle in our deception.

We accumulate disciples, ministries, and converts. Small

groups are a success when the living room has no empty seats left. Baptisms are the ultimate celebration of achievement in the life of the missionary. Running from ministry to ministry all day every day is a sign of maturity in the believer. This must stop. We have to stop.

We are trampling the blind. They cannot keep up. What is worse is that we don't even notice their blindness as they cling to us hoping to hang on long enough to make it to the other side of the road. Instead of being efficient as Jesus was (I mean He fed over 5,000 people with 5 loaves of bread and 2 fish, talk about efficiency), we are just in a hurry. As long as we fall into bed exhausted every night we have achieved success or so we think. We desperately need to stop long enough to re-examine the life of the One we seek to imitate.

What if we allowed Jesus's life to set the pace? What if we set aside—just for a moment—our personalities and the culture that surrounds us? Let us silence the inner voice that demands more, faster, and admit that in our frenzied hurry we are missing out on the blind man right beside us. Let's allow God to define efficiency.

JESUS SETS THE PACE

Reading about the life of Jesus, I notice that He was never in a hurry. Because of that, He had the ability to live in each moment without His attention being pulled somewhere else. This is significant. He had plenty of reasons to be distracted throughout the years of His ministry, but He chose focus. I am distracted all the time. I sit with a friend to have coffee and instead of engaging in what she says, I think about what

I need to do when I get back home.

Jesus was so different. He somehow lived His life distraction-free, while maintaining very specific goals. He knew what He had come to earth to do. He knew that Jerusalem was His destination. He knew that He was on earth to proclaim the kingdom of heaven and to heal the sick. He preached, discipled, healed, traveled, and evangelized, all the while remaining attentive to the ever-changing needs and people around Him.

Somehow, Jesus kept moving toward Jerusalem with His feet and His heart, but stopped to weep at the grave of a lost friend. He was not thrown off by the chaos of the crowd pushing in on Him as He made His way to heal a sick girl. He even stopped to talk to the woman who touched His robe. Somehow, He noticed her, but at the same time did not forget about the girl and where He was going.

I probably would have tried to shake off the lady as I had the man at the traffic light in a hurry to get to the girl. He always saw the people that the Lord had put right in front of Him. He saw every blind man every time.

Jesus committed Himself to enter into the story of each person who sought His attention. It might have been a short interaction for some of them, but each time we read about someone who sought the attention of Jesus, we see that he or she received it.

Some sought His attention to trick Him and He still gave it to them, but Jesus wisely pierced through their smooth words and revealed their impure motives. He gave His attention to children who sought it and to women who needed it. Social norms were often ignored as He interacted with the unclean and the "unworthy."

Not once did He seem bothered or annoyed that these people kept crying out to Him and taking His time away from other things. He gave Himself to each situation as it came with perfect wisdom. It is true that we will never do this with the perfection that belongs to Jesus alone, but is not the same Spirit available to guide us? Our call to enter into the world around us demands that we silence distraction.

RE-WIRING MY BRAIN TO SLOW DOWN

I have developed a new habit in the last couple of months. When I make a 'to-do list', even a mental one, I cut it in half. Then, I cut it in half again. I am finding that the remaining twenty-five percent is a more realistic picture of what I can accomplish for that day or week.

Then, I pray that the Lord would open my eyes and my heart to those who will come beside me throughout the day. I try to be aware of the people I see as I go work through my list. I stop to talk to those I recognize, even if just for a couple of minutes. I slow down as I ask for wisdom to see others. I try to answer texts, if not urgent, when I have free time and not in the moment they arrive. These choices are all attempts to minimize distraction. These ideas are my ways to cut down on hurry in order to be more present. Feel free to borrow mine, or come up with a few of your own.

I am tired of walking through life distracted, missing the people right in front of me. I long to have both the laser-focus of Jesus and also the freedom to stop for those who come into my path. I am tired of shaking off the arm of the person that is just trying to cross the street. I want to enter into his story by noticing him and walking with him until he continues his way.

For this I need wisdom, but that is already promised to me if I would but ask. So what am I waiting for? Think of all the people Jesus met along the way. He gave them undivided attention and care. Think of all the ways Jesus worked for the Father's will and pleasure. Imagine what is in store for us if we are willing to imitate Jesus. Imagine what is available to the attentive. Learn from my mistake. If someone grabs your arm, look to see why.

Things Worth Remembering
- *Get off the phone*
- *Notice the people around you*
- *Let Jesus set the pace*
- *Small attentive moments = entering into the story of another*
- *Stop the frenzy of hurry*

Getting settled in Bishkek

A bus stop in Kyrgyzstan—A
good reminder to slow down

Chapter 4:

ADDITIONAL NEEDS & LANGUAGE BRAIN

My emotions drained, my willpower gone
I stare ahead. I'm numb.

That encounter at the traffic light occurred during my six months of living in Bishkek, Kyrgyzstan. After that I spent three years at a Bible College in Hungary and then stood before not only a new border, and a new language, but also a new boyfriend: soon to be husband. I felt assured that crossing over was not something I was pushing, but was another transplanted desire of Someone greater. Since crossing that border on February 14, 2011, my heart has grown roots never to detach.

PLUMB LINE OF THE HEART

What I did not know, was that a plumb line would be dropped over the top of my self-drawn path, revealing more of the crookedness within. Thankfully, I didn't know. That knowledge would have been too much, too soon.

A plumb line is a tool that is used to determine if something is vertically straight. Anything not straight must be knocked down or ripped off and built again. We all know what happens if the truth of the plumb line is ignored; the distortion continues and the instability increases leaving a dangerous, useless wall teetering in the lightest breeze.

If, however, the wisdom of the plumb line is taken and a skilled hand engaged, the crookedness can be removed. New brick can replace the old, rebuilding strength and restoring usefulness. This sounds simple enough—and it is—but it is not without pain to the wall. If a wall could talk, it would cry out as the crooked bricks were torn away from the mortar holding them fast together. It would be a cry of pain. It is not a crooked wall on top of a straight one, but one wall; straight and crooked all cemented together. Carelessness could knock down the straight with the crooked, but a wise builder will only knock down that which is not useful and leave that which is. He uses his tool to reveal what is true and then removes what is not. He will enrich the wall in the end, if He is allowed to work.

I was up to the challenge. You see, I thought that I was the plumb line and the builder, coming in to make straight what was crooked. I was finally going to live in a foreign country, not just until I figured out what was next or until I finished my studies, but forever. I was finally going to get the chance to tell the truth to those who had never heard. Having known the True and Faithful even as a young child left me feeling like an expert in all things pertaining to the truth and I had dedicated my life to proclaiming and spreading this truth.

STARTING TO LIVE AND STARTING TO TALK

So, with the lessons of no-man's-land held close to my heart, I immigrated to a new place. I knew the overwhelming process of learning a new language and the grit it took to keep trying. This would be my third foreign language attempt, not including High School French. I knew that everything would be different and unfamiliar and I knew that ultimately, I was not making this move for myself. I was answering the summons of a Voice that I was committed to follow.

I was nervous about moving, probably because of all that I had learned, but brushed that aside. I did feel a little bit unsure of myself as I unpacked my bags, but I reasoned that these nervous moments were nothing out of the ordinary. It was as if I chose to wear short-sleeves without realizing how chilly the morning air was, but I remained unconcerned knowing that the sun would come out as the day progressed. At least I wasn't naked, or so I thought.

Settling into a new place takes time. Our feet run fast, leaving the heart dragging behind and so when the feet stop, the heart must catch up. In some ways, our hearts are always playing catch-up in this fast-paced, activity-addicted world. My heart was working overtime in that first year. I left friends behind and with them the life of being a student.

I crossed not only the border into Serbia, but also the invisible border into adulthood. I was living in a city I had visited once for a weekend. In all, I knew exactly two people. My future husband and my roommate, both indigenous, leaving me as the only gringo.

I started language lessons right away with a teacher who spoke no English. These lessons put me on the fast track to learn Serbian well. However, I was also headed toward a mental breakdown. Many lessons left me thinking that I would never learn to speak well enough to live a normal adult life.

I pushed on, determined to one day be able to share about the love of the Voice who called me to this new place and to share in the heart language of those around me. I wanted them to know that I was trying to respect my new home and had been told that learning their language was a good place to start. It was overwhelming from day one. My then boyfriend took the brunt of my emotional instability and wiped the majority of my tears. He was my rock, which was convenient considering I was madly in love with him. What I did not love was his suggestion that we start volunteering at a club for adults with additional needs.

This club would be a social event, which meant talking. Talking meant Serbian. Serbian meant that I would morph into a toddler; desperate to be understood but only able to babble. After the first visit my fears were confirmed. In my mind it was a disaster.

I had taken enough language lessons to begin to understand the Slavic sounds being spoken around me. I could go the local Farmers Market and ask how much a vegetable cost and usually understand the answer. I would study my numbers to a hundred and the name of one vegetable and then set off on my crusade. The triumph of setting carrots on the table at home was satisfying, but it took days to make even a simple soup.

Nevertheless, I was learning. I even knew all my letters. Painstakingly, I had sat at my living room table with a preschool workbook tracing out each letter until I could write it and recognize it. My roommate's mother laughed so hard when she came in one day and saw what I was doing. She kissed me and rattled off some combination of those letters that I couldn't find in my book. Some days, my brain shut down completely. It was the blue screen of death under my eyelids. Other days, I felt good and would try to communicate and use my new knowledge to engage in life around me.

Once a week, though, at that club, I was forced to interact whether I wanted to or not. It was a massive struggle every week that never got easier. I never started enjoying it. The concept behind the club was to provide a safe place for adults with additional needs to hang out. There was little structure and a lot of talking. It was impossible for me to understand those who had a speaking impediment, were missing teeth, whose speech did not follow a logical flow, or those who spoke too fast. You can imagine, then, how much I was understanding: close to nothing. I felt like a burden, and definitely not the star volunteer that I wanted to be.

REALITY CHECK

I thought it couldn't get worse. I was being stripped down to the core of who I was and operating on the level of a two-year-old. My body was protesting all the stress and I was so exhausted that I was sure I had mono. Off to the doctor I went, with my boyfriend Danny of course, because he had to help me get there, talk there and get me home after my appointment. All doubt vanished when I could barely walk up the stairs at the clinic. My blood work came back perfect. I was a picture of resplendent health. Later, I would learn about a thing called culture stress and a lot of things would make more sense, but at that time I just felt tired even down to my bones.

Back to the club I went, no doctor's note to excuse my absence. Danny and I played games with the attendees and participated in all the activities. I sat and listened, understanding some, but was unable to respond quickly enough to verbally interact. One evening, while there, I overheard one of the participants talking to Danny,

"How come I can speak Hungarian and Serbian and English and she can't even speak Serbian?" He was looking at me.

Anger rose up within me and embarrassment colored my

cheeks. *I am smart. You just can't see it. I could talk circles around you in English.* Not being able to say it out loud in Serbian didn't stop the thoughts from forming.

Looking back, I don't think that he was being mean or trying to make fun of me. I think that he was genuinely confused about the fact that he had a mental impairment, but knew more than me, a person who was supposedly mentally superior. He wanted to know how it was possible that he was smarter than I was.

The embarrassment I felt was magnified by the truth of his words. It *was* true that he had more knowledge of Serbian than I did. It *was* true that he spoke more languages. It *was* true that he, in these ways, was mentally superior to me. It was logical for him to be confused by this.

My inner self fought hard to regain my superior status, but had no case to present. The plumb line had been held up and had revealed a shameful type of crookedness that exalts self above all others and revels in the superiority. I never would have said it, nor did I realize that I thought it, but I truly believed that I was better than this man.

Do you see the crookedness? Can you smell the stench? I believed that, because I happened to be born with a typically developing mind, I was a better human than he, who happened to be born with a mind that refused to progress past a certain point. Stop for a moment and read that sentence again and allow your nostrils to inhale and process the stink.

It's humiliating to write this story because it's true. The thoughts in my mind were a part of me. Just like the things about me that were good and right, the crookedness lived there, too, and that realization hurt. Those bricks of pride were mortared together right along with the other ones. For the first time, I saw how they jutted out. Actually, they didn't jut out and that was the problem. It was a slow leaning that eventually gave way to crookedness and so it took a long time to notice. Noticing was grace.

Just as that man was not trying to embarrass or belittle me, neither was the One orchestrating those events. I don't believe that it was by accident that I overheard that conversation, nor that I understood the words spoken. I believe that it was grace. I believe that the Master Builder was prepping the wall. He saw structural instability and He desired to fix it.

He did not thrust the plumb line at me screaming, "Does this look straight to you? Do you think I can use a wall like this? Look at all the wasted brick that I have to tear out!" No, that is a different voice; one you should run from as soon as it starts its rant.

Gentleness is His way, but that does not mean that He will overlook those dangerous bricks and He also doesn't always wait for convenient times to reveal the state of our hearts. I was in an extremely vulnerable state. I was being crushed by language learning through immersion, feeling emotional, overwhelmed, and lost. But He still went ahead with the hard work of freeing me from my destructive self. He does not share in our deceptions, but sees crookedness for what it is.

Do you think that I could ever treat that man with the respect and honor that he deserves as my equal when I thought I was better than him? Could I genuinely open my heart to him in friendship with such a superiority complex? Would I be open to learn Serbian from him with such pride lurching in my heart? No, no, and no. Do you think I could worship, out of a pure heart, the One who created that man and allowed him to say what he did while in my crooked state? Absolutely not.

The Builder knows that pride destroys relationships. It erects itself high above every other, ignoring the fact that the higher it gets, the more distorted it becomes. He holds up that line in order to restore. He is willing to knock down and then commit Himself to painstakingly rebuild: brick by brick. The extra effort is not an issue as patient love does its work.

KNOWING ISN'T EVERYTHING

Change is possible and a rebuilt straight wall is so much better than a crooked one. This became clear when I found myself, once again, volunteering at a club for adults with additional needs; a different club in a different city, but with most of the same challenges. I did have more language skills, but every visit was still difficult. One time, I was sitting with a lady and we were watching a Soap Opera in Turkish, another language that I do not know. I didn't understand even one word. It had Serbian subtitles, but they were changing so fast that it was impossible for me to follow the story. The lady next to me was smiling and clearly enjoying the episode.

"Are they speaking Turkish?" I asked in Serbian.

She nodded.

"I wish I could follow the story," I said. "The words change so fast. I'm so confused about what is going on. I can't read fast enough."

She turned her head toward me and smiled, "I can't read

at all!"

We both laughed out loud and the sprout of friendship popped up out of the soil of my new freedom to be me, whatever knowledge I may or may not possess. We watched the episode until it finished: curiosity trumping comprehension.

<u>Things Worth Remembering</u>
- Strange people and strange places = spike in humility
- You will, at some point, be embarrassed
- Open yourself to the idea that it can be the source of growth
- Don't run
- Allow yourself to be rebuilt

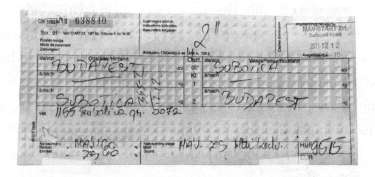

Ticket to my new home in
Subotica, Serbia

The farmer's market where I
practiced ordering vegetables in
Serbian

Chapter 5:

COCKROACHES &
PRESSED SLACKS

Everything glows a different hue
Under their shadowy haze.

SLOBO

It was absolutely filthy, not that I was surprised, so was he. The first time I met Slobo, he had a large stain on his pants suggesting that his bowel control might be lacking. His shirt and face were streaked with dirt and he stank. It seemed fitting that we met next to a dumpster: one that he was digging through to find food. I shyly handed him banana bread and invited him to come have coffee at our church the next morning, glad that Danny, not me, would be the one waiting for him there.

The next morning came and went without him. I wasn't surprised. I had thought he would be like all the others I had given bread to and invited for coffee. None of them came either–but unlike them–he had promised to come. Unlike them–something about him drew me in, which meant that I was looking forward to finding out more of his story.

He had been genuinely friendly when I met him and grateful for the bread. Often people rejected it without question. Or if they did take the bread it was with downcast eyes: not Slobo. He had thanked me and talked with me for a few minutes, joking about something, his eyes meeting mine. We were equal. There was nothing intimidating about him, except for the stench, a stench which was strangely lacking in his friend who was standing next to him. The two men had nothing in common.

Slobo was the epitome of homeless: he embodied neglect as his person was covered in filth. The man standing right next to him digging through the same dumpster was wearing a dress shirt and pressed slacks. Everything about him suggested a love of cleanliness and attention to detail. His hands weren't even dirty.

I wanted details. How? Why? When? What? And where? Of course, I didn't want to be the one asking those questions, nor did I have a great desire to spend any length of time with these men. That's where Danny would come in handy.

He is great at asking questions, much better than I am, so my plan was for him to hang out with them and then come home and tell me all the juicy details. This perfect arrangement would save me all of the awkwardness that comes with meeting new people and actually attempting to get to know them: an awkwardness that becomes magnified when the talking and getting to know is in a second language. They would come to coffee, receive what we had to offer, tell their stories, maybe hear a little about Jesus, and be on their way. It was the perfect ministry: no long-term investment required: no messy attempts at conversation in my non-native language. I had it all figured out.

Eventually though, somewhere along the way, my plans went terribly wrong and I found myself sitting in Slobo's apartment. Was it as unkempt as his appearance? Yes. It was absolutely filthy and I loved being there. Slobo was no longer a random stranger, but our friend. An unlikely one and as it turned out not homeless, as hard as that was to believe.

He lived in a little apartment with his wife and it was in that place that was so familiar to him that he started to talk. He slowly began to tell us his story and over many visits and several months, his stained pants and yellowed walls began to make more sense.

It was a story earned mostly by Danny, as he listened to

Slobo. Yes, he finally came to our church one morning for coffee. In fact, not just for coffee, but also for Bible studies. Slobo became a regular and never came alone. He always showed up with three, sometimes four, other homeless-looking guys in tow.

In the mornings, when he came, he and Danny would drink coffee, talk, and read some verses from the Bible. Then, one day it happened. He invited us over.

There is something about being invited into someone's home. Entering a place where someone is usually most at ease is like entering into a part of their soul. A home is often an extension of the person who lives there, even if the furniture is not to their taste. The atmosphere of the home points to something about its dwellers: subtle or not.

At Slobo's, his influence was not subtle, but then again nothing about him was. The first visit was a shock even though it turned out to be just what I had expected. The dirt on the floor was so thickly caked on that the floor's actual color was left entirely up to my imagination. The furniture was minimal: two couches, a small coffee table, a dresser, a stove, a mini fridge, and one cupboard comprised everything.

There were no pictures on any of the walls. A cheap heart-shaped pillow that said "I love you" sat on the couch opposite me. On the dresser to the right sat several knickknacks, most of them broken, obvious finds during his dumpster digging.

As we sat drinking coffee from mugs that I doubt had ever been touched by soap and eating snacks that were also found in a dumpster, there sat Slobo, drinking a beer and talking about how he only had one glass a day, two at the most. He swore that he drank because he liked the taste and could stop anytime he wanted; this was an assurance we never asked for.

HOPE?

The glass or two of beer, the walls, that floor, all revealed pieces of Slobo that I just couldn't understand at first. There is a well-known phrase in English which reflects its speakers' mentality more than they may realize. "Hope springs eternal," we say. There is always a reason to hope is what we mean.

You persevere and fight through life, holding on to the hope that things will one day get better. Springs are a place of refreshment and life and the hope-spring never dries up. All you have to do is go and dip your cup in and get some hope for yourself. Hope is always available. It is always flowing, waiting to be utilized.

That all sounds very nice and inspiring in English. English was not Slobo's heart language and I doubt he had ever heard that phrase, but his language also has a phrase about hope. "Hope dies last".

The first time I heard that phrase I laughed and thought *well, that's depressing.* Hope. Dies. Last. The insinuation is that even though hope can hang on longer than anything else, it will eventually go the way of all other living things. It will die.

The struggle and heaviness of this simple phrase reflects a mentality of fighting to survive and shouldering burdens that never go away. Everything—even hope—will eventually be lost. Slobo's life embodied this phrase and for the first time I was confronted with a dried-up spring.

How could he not care about anything? How could a person

who is perfectly sane walk around the city and come to Bible studies with a poop stain and cockroaches crawling out of his shirt? I was baffled. He was a likable guy. He knew when to talk, when to ask questions, and when to listen. If there was an awkward conversationalist in the room it wasn't him. He was intelligent, liked to joke and tease and was hopeless, really hopeless. Once again, my nosiness took over.

Why? Maybe it's laziness? Can a person really be that lazy? Somehow, it didn't feel like laziness in his home though. It was different. He had the same look as an animal as it paces its cage in the zoo. A look of utter complacency and submission to their fate of a hopeless existence in captivity.

Slobo's cage had many bars I would learn: war, death, insanity, racism. You name it, he lived through it. These events left him completely hopeless. He was pacing, complacent, with a drink in hand. I found myself pushing back against this lack of hope. "It doesn't have to be this way," I wanted to shout. I wanted to analyze, problem-solve, troubleshoot until Slobo too was drinking from the spring of my ever-flowing hope.

I wanted to pull him over to the water and force a cupful down his throat, but life doesn't work that way. For him, hope had died. This was his world. There was no spring. I couldn't point him toward something that for him didn't exist. I couldn't change his perception of reality. The only thing that I could do was to enter into his perception and attempt to feel what he felt.

STAINS AND EMPATHY

Of course, I couldn't do this entirely since I had not experienced what he had, but I tried to allow the weight of it to hit me. I could enter his world of no hope and sit in it with him.

Not forever and not allowing it to replace my reality and dry up my spring, but long enough. Long enough to push understanding as far as I could. Long enough to suffer with him. I actually don't think that much pushing was even necessary for me to get a glimpse.

That close—sitting on the couch opposite him—his suffering leapt out at me and enveloped me. One picture was all it took really. It was a picture of Slobo's home and he was standing in front of it, arms draped around his father and brother. It was not the home I was sitting in. It was his real home, the one he was forced out of because he was the wrong tribe. He had lost everything. Suddenly, the stains on the walls became of no importance.

To run for your life once is horrible enough, but to run for your life and settle in another country only to run for your life again 10 years later is unimaginable. Slobo never talked about the things he saw as he ran, but whatever they were, they broke his brother's sanity. Slobo had no money to visit him in the insane asylum even though it was only a 2-hour drive away. As if that wasn't enough, he also watched his father get sick and die in his own apartment. Hope had been stripped away from him bit by bit until there was not even a hint of it left. Hope died last.

War-torn is not limited to the state of a country. It can

just as easily be the state of a soul. War had left so many scars in Slobo that the man in the picture I held in my hand had very little in common with the man I now knew. I wish I could have jumped into that picture and gotten to know the Slobo before captivity. Sometimes I got glimpses of what he must have been like through his witty humor and kindness, but those moments never lasted long. Hopelessness always had the last word, but instead of fighting this, I learned to respect that he was being genuine. He was sharing his life honestly with me. That is something I could learn to do better with those around me. Even if it makes others uncomfortable, my relationships would be deeper if there was this kind of honest 2-way sharing.

On one visit, however, I noticed something new next to that heart-shaped pillow; a red New Testament, a gift from us. He told us that he read it and would like to read it together. So we did. Not every visit, but sometimes.

Sometimes he just talked about his life and that picture, but other times we opened that book and read a part of the grandest story of all: a story of hope resurrected. It is impossible to know how deep that story penetrated into Slobo's heart.

I'm afraid I will never know if his hope was resurrected, as he was taken from us suddenly after a bad fall. But that little red book received a place in his home. A place of display even, sitting where all could see it. I hold on to that, hoping that, as it had won a place in his home, maybe it had also won a place in his heart.

MILOVAN

It was that same history of loss that linked those unlikely friends from the dumpster. I would learn that those two men were not as different as they looked. I now know that a war-torn soul can be dressed in meticulously taken-care-of clothing just as easily as it can be covered in dirt.

Milovan's appearance was also an extension of his home. His apartment was clean and orderly. Soap was used in my presence to carefully wash each coffee mug immediately after use. Curtains were hung and pictures were on the walls and yet leaving Milovan's place left me with the same feeling as leaving Slobo's. Thinking back, I don't remember being actually present when he told his story. I think he told Danny and Danny told me. Either way, somehow, sitting with him to drink coffee over and over again, his emotional walls came down and he shared his greatest heartbreak. We already knew some of the smaller ones. A wife he never talked about and an estranged daughter. But like Slobo, war had dealt him the biggest blow.

Milovan's son had been stationed where the war was the cruelest, and though his son came home, he was not the same. He survived, but could not come to terms with what he had seen. Eventually his son took his own life.

Milovan's only son, his heir and the only immediate family member Milovan was still in relationship with, shot himself. He shot himself with Milovan's gun.

While Milovan expressed his pain in hopelessness different than Slobo's, his grief had the same crushing weight. Milovan said that he hung out with Slobo in an attempt to help him stop drinking and get back on his feet. Milovan walked the streets collecting wooden fruit crates left next to dumpsters in order to sell them. He made a little money, which he needed, and sometimes found edibles among the trash, but more than anything it was a reason to get out of his apartment and out of his head. He was much more upbeat in general than Slobo, but as we got to know him I realized he wasn't that different from the one he sought to help.

The confusion I felt that first day of our happenstance meeting next to the garbage was fading. These friends were united in a world of pain and refused to acknowledge that there was a way out. Not a way out as in an escape, but a way to plant seeds that would allow new growth: healthy plants to bring oxygen and nourishment to depleted hearts gasping for breath.

That is what hopelessness really does. It closes us off to newness: the newness that comes with the change of the seasons, the newness that comes with the sowing of seeds. Hope sows with expectation, anticipating that the thing being waited for will satisfy the longing of our hearts. Hope helps us on our journeys to be whole.

Pieces of Slobo had been taken from him all along the way and he longed to have them back. He longed to be restored to what he once was. Milovan longs for what he once had to be restored to him. Slobo's longing was never met. Milovan's longings will never be realized and so hopelessness has taken root. It has filled the ground until there is no room for anything to grow. It has stolen all the soil so that new seeds lay on the surface and wait to be devoured by birds. Hopelessness has taken over like a thorny vine, slowly deteriorating the heart.

It chokes and squeezes.

UNDERSTANDING HOPE SLAIN

There is a beautiful Cornelian cherry tree next to our family cabin. It is the first to bloom in the spring, a burst of yellow sets the landscape ablaze with color after a barren winter. Its leaves then grow and give us shade to sit under. Its branches hold our hammock. Its cherries are used for nourishment. It is beautiful to look at and very useful, but it does have one problem.

All along one side of it grows a thorny vine. This nasty vine reaches up and pulls the branches drown, wrapping itself around them, stealing their sun and choking away their life. To stop the destruction, each individual vine must be cut back or else the branches will dry up in its clutches. To cut them, I have to get really close to see where each vine starts its anaconda squeeze. I have to pull it back from the branch as I cut it away so that I don't damage the branch I am trying to save. I have to work slowly, freeing one branch at a time and I have to get as close as I can to the thorns so I can see what I am doing.

Even though I am careful, at some point I will scratch myself on the thorns. Being that close, surrounded by the spikey barbs, it is only a matter of time before one comes into contact with my skin. The scratches are not life threatening, but they sting. Even when their marks fade, my mind remembers the pain. So why do I draw near to those thorns?

It's simple really, I hate seeing that remarkable tree with its branches twisted and broken. I feel bad for it, even if it's just a tree. So I get my shears and gloves and go to work. It's actually compassion's fault that my arms get all cut up. If I didn't feel for my tree, I would not open myself up to the attack of the thorns. If I did not love the tree, I would have stopped my campaign against the vine after the first scratch or two.

Even though my crusade to save my tree came years after meeting Slobo and Milovan, the similarity between these men and my tree is striking. They were beautiful people and I had begun to care about them and so had also grown to hate the thorny clutches of hopelessness pulling them down. It was unpleasant and painful to enter into their worlds, and I was left with scratches, but somehow didn't want to run away. I wanted to move closer, to understand better. I wanted to feel more, and the more I felt their pain, the more I grew to love them and just like I freed my tree, I wanted to free them. I wanted to get my shears out and get to work, cutting away the vines, but I couldn't. Hopelessness is a thorny vine that only one pair of shears can cut through. My tiny shears don't stand a chance and so I learned that compassion is not about fixing a situation or a state of being. It's about presence. While I could not cut away their despair or resurrect their hope, I could sit next to them and trust that the One who Himself was resurrected was sitting there as well, shears in hand. I could not change their reality, but I could carry a different one within myself and, as we sat side by side, pray that they would notice.

Compassion is suffering with someone, it's not becoming them. I do have scratches, but my hope is very much still alive and that hope is just as much for them as it is for me. I know that hope can be resurrected, so I sit and wait. I might not see the glorious moment with my own eyes, but trust the Gardener. He wastes no opportunity and His longing to free the captives is vastly larger than mine. I believe that He was cutting away at Slobo's choking vines until his last breath and still continues to offer hope resurrected to Milovan.

Hope dying last doesn't make me laugh anymore. It now has a face. The realities that Slobo and Milovan chose to live in are completely logical considering their life experiences. This is something I had never considered before getting to know these incredible men. But spending time with them and listening to them, not to replace their realities with mine but to understand them better, led me on a journey with hope. Hope is more complicated for me now and at times makes me uncomfortable and even confused. There is a tension that was not present before.

I now know that hope can die, but at the same time still hear the gurgle of the spring. But how can that be? These two realities can't coexist. Or can they? Haven't they for over 2,000 years? My heart knows the story of that red New Testament sitting on the back of the couch. It is the story of hope, but as with any story, the timeline is everything. The story is of hope dying and then springing back to life: life eternal. Saying that Jesus is our hope only holds power because He has been resurrected, but before that happened, He was slain. Hope did die, but the gurgle couldn't be silenced and He took His life up again, reemerging from the grave, never to return. The tension might always remain but, just like in Jesus, these two phrases can coexist in us. Hope can die last, and the miracle of its resurrection can spring eternal. For me, this tension brings a better understanding for those on the death side. A willingness to sit with them and feel hope die has been born in me and instead of this threatening my hope, I see now that it enriches it.

Things Worth Remembering
- Press in; initiate the friendship
- Listen and suffer with
- Hope dies last
- Hope springs eternal

Our beautiful Cornelian
cherry tree

'Bible Club,' where Danny and
Slobo would sometimes have
coffee

Chapter 6:

ENTERING TO EXIT

Something new has grasped my heart,
A wonder words can't convey.

Not all living rooms are gateways to such marvel. I am learning that having compassion, which is only possible by getting close enough to feel the suffering of another, is dependent on the others' willingness to share themselves.

It isn't easy to share your life with others. Milovan and Slobo were brave to share their stories with us in such a raw and unfiltered way. It was their willingness to be vulnerable that made our compassion possible. We could begin to understand them because they allowed us to. They boldly let us see the real them. Some living rooms are not so honest.

Danny and I had been invited over, not just for coffee but to read the Bible with an entire family. A phone conversation with the only son not living at home left us convinced that everyone was excited to meet us. The parents were even willing to open up their home for a weekly home group, a time for the family to study the Bible with their neighbors.

This was the first time we had encountered such openness and we were praising the Lord for it. I was already envisioning a packed living room, everyone crowded around, desperate to hear the Word of God. I could even make cookies. This was the beginning of the revival we had been praying for.

Danny listened to my vision as we drove to the house and wisely said, "Let's visit first and take it one step at a time. There's no need to rush."

I wasn't deterred though. Once I get an idea, I usually start running with it. Sometimes I run to new and exciting places, spurring on those around me. And sometimes I run right into a brick wall.

Not all my ideas are from the Lord and so not all of them hold the power to accelerate and inspire. This mini revival, as you will see, was an idea of the second kind. I hit that brick wall at a full run, but instead of hurting me, the wall taught me.

I was about to experience the Lord use me in a way that I had never felt before. I would see Him use a part of my personality that I thought was useless in His kingdom. I should have known better.

God wastes nothing and redeems everything. Zero waste, 100% recycled material is stamped on all His creation. That was the first lesson. I was also about to learn that without honesty, it's impossible to enter into a meaningful relationship. Authenticity is the real foundation of friendship.

We rang the doorbell. I was smiling—my vision at the forefront of my mind. A young lady came to greet us and invited us to come in. We walked through the open door both literally and figuratively.

I shouted, "Praise the Lord for you all. You are an answer to our prayers. I can't wait to see how many people will come to this house to hear the Word of our Lord." Well, my mind shouted these things, but, thankfully, my mouth stayed closed.

We took off our shoes and moved from the hallway into the living room. My eye immediately landed on the huge family Bible sitting on the table. *Wow, that's big,* I thought.

The mother motioned for us to sit down at the table as she laid down the book she was reading. It was a devotional of some sort.

"Coffee?" she asked.

"Always," our reply.

The daughter went to the stove to make us each a cup of

strong Turkish coffee.

First, we were introduced to the middle son. He shook each of our hands while holding a small Bible in the free one. He had apparently been reading it before we arrived. The youngest son was next, sitting on the couch, also holding a Bible.

Wow, that's a lot of Bibles. The thought shot through my mind before I could stop it. *We have just as many Bibles at our house,* now I was arguing with myself. *Yeah, but they are never all out at the same time. Maybe they're doing family devotions. Focus, Wendy.* I blinked hard in an attempt to come back to reality. The blink must have unplugged my ears because all of the sudden I heard music, softly playing in the background. It was Christian worship music and it added another layer of piety to the Bible-filled room.

The father came into the room next, introduced himself and sat down. We drank coffee and talked for some time. Everyone seemed excited about the Bible study and each one had a story about something that God had done in their life.

It was inspiring, or rather it should have been. But for some reason it wasn't and I couldn't figure out why. For some reason, it felt like we had walked into a movie set instead of into an actual living room. It all felt a bit staged.

Now, we also play soft music in the background when guests come over and often it is Christian music. There have also been times when a Bible was left out on the table. We sit and have coffee with people all the time in similar settings, but this wasn't like those times. It was weird. I felt bad even thinking such thoughts until Danny shared similar observations on the way home. He is usually perceptive, so it was significant to me that he sensed something was off too.

STORIES OF OLD

The family kept inviting us over and we kept going, but somehow, we never got around to studying the Bible. There were always stories of something that they had done for the Lord and always vague references to passages they had read, but that strange feeling from the first visit never stopped. We couldn't figure out what it was though, so we kept going over.

Slowly, the more time we spent in that living room, the more we started getting a different picture, a more accurate picture of what was really going on.

I have no idea how many visits it took me to realize that the stories I was hearing, especially from the mom, were always the same few stories, but it was a lot.

These stories were all set several years before our visits began and they were always rotated through. There was always at least one Bible or devotional on the table and how impactful it had been was always mentioned. A strange thing happened, however, when we probed deeper about what exactly it was that had been so impactful—no one could remember what they had read.

Other details were surfacing as well, thanks to that son who no longer lived at home. The picture he painted was very different than what we were experiencing in person. There was past trouble with the law and even current trouble with the law, resulting from things done during the time we had been going over to their house, but they had never mentioned those troubles.

This son mentioned alcohol addiction and violence, all coinciding with the period of time our meetings took place, but strangely that was neither mentioned nor lifted up before the Lord in prayer. The only things that had been mentioned were health problems, but there was no evidence of lifestyle change or a concrete plan to change habits.

Of course, it's not to be expected that these kinds of sensitive, personal things would be shared right away, but as the family continued to insist that they were actively seeking and receiving from the Lord, the red flags started popping up. The impression that they were giving through their words and home environment turned out to be a facade to distract from the real state of their family.

I don't want to give you the impression that I dreaded going over to sit in that living room, but I began to have an underlying frustration. Oddly enough, I was not frustrated about the alcohol or the law-breaking or the lack of discipline. Those were all things that I had seen the Lord free his children, myself included, from. I knew those issues were no match for the power of the Spirit.

What was frustrating was that week after week we sat talking about how they had given all the food in their fridge away to hungry neighbors four years ago. Four years ago. And yet, what was read that same morning could not even be recalled. I was frustrated that all those Bibles didn't appear to be affecting any of their everyday lives.

Danny shared in my frustration and we talked about it often, but were unsure what we should do. So, we kept visiting and praying for them. We wanted them to know that we were available and genuinely willing to walk through hard things with them. We wanted to give them time. Depth must be earned and there was no need to rush.

I sometimes hung out with the daughter and Danny met regularly with the middle son. I tried to connect with the daughter about the things of the Lord, knowing that no matter how different we were, there can always be fellowship in the Spirit. I never really felt that connection with her, though. Talking about the Lord was difficult and I was always the one to initiate that topic. I couldn't tell if she enjoyed hanging out with me or valued me as a person. It felt like the relationship wasn't progressing. I know what you're thinking—that line is what someone says before a breakup. Yes it is: and with good reason.

Danny began to learn from the oldest brother that the brother he was meeting with was being less than honest. Danny tried to talk to him about it. He wanted to meet with him to hang out and study the Bible, but without honesty there was no point. This is something Danny tried to explain. The brother exploded, yelling and shouting as if the tone of his voice would convince Danny he wasn't lying.

THE TIPPING POINT

Then, we hit the brick wall. We were once again sitting at that table surrounded by Bibles and I felt the Lord leading me to confront the mom about the stories and vagueness. I didn't want to, and even more than not wanting to, I was afraid to.

I had confronted people in the past and it had not ended well. Even that word "confront" makes all of the air leak out of my lungs, leaving me deflated.

I had confronted people in anger and with harshness and it had ripped through the relationship like a forest fire. In the past, I was direct and rough and I wasn't sure I could keep the directness without that sting of harshness.

Someone had even told me, "Wendy you are as wise as a serpent but not as gentle as a dove." Ouch.

He was not giving me a compliment and in my heart, I knew that though this statement stung, it was true. In the past, I had not thought about what it would be like to receive such words, but only about defending the truth. Back then, I didn't have any problem offending someone if it meant I could defend the truth, but I was changing. I was tired of hurting people. I was beginning to understand how hard it can be to face such direct language. So, what was my solution? I kept my mouth shut and listened to this lady over and over again.

That visit though, I just couldn't do it anymore. There's another breakup line for you. The amazing thing was that unlike all those times in the past, I wasn't angry or even frustrated at the mom. I wasn't satisfied with the state of our relationship, lack of depth and what I thought was insincerity, but I was not mad at any member of that family.

This helped me discern that the Spirit was working. I believe that the Lord had shown me how desperately He wanted to do something new in the mom's life and how He longed to add to her repertoire of stories: new ventures of faith. He was seeking to uncover the hidden things in order to heal and make straight what was crooked. Remember the wall? Not the one I ran into, the one from before? I felt like He was calling me, in that moment, to drop the plumb line. I knew it had a lot to reveal, and I was afraid to do it, but decided to trust the Voice.

I started asking questions. I was extra careful to be kind and gentle, knowing myself and my tendencies from the past. Instead of plowing through to the truth that her relationship with the Lord was based on the past and not the present, I tried to slowly lead her to that realization inch by inch.

I will never forget that conversation. Not because it resulted in an amazing miracle or an instant breakthrough. It did not end in either of those things. It actually ended the relationship entirely because the words I shared were rejected, met by a wall of other sorts.

Ended it for now, I should say. Paused it. If any of those people came to me to renew our friendship, I would say yes. I would try again, which is evidence of the change being wrought in me. Gentleness and grace go hand-in-hand. Yes, they would need to regain my trust, but if they were open and honest, I would meet those efforts, not because I am an amazing person, but because that is what Jesus would do and did.

PROMPTS OF THE SPIRIT

As I read about His life, I notice a pattern. Equal attention was given to each person He met, but the depth and length of the relationship was up to the person and not Jesus. Jesus never rejected people. I can't think of one time that He ignored or walked away from a person who was pursuing Him, but He did confront hypocrisy.

Hypocrisy is a form of dishonesty with an extra helping of pride. Jesus addressed the absence of truth in the statements and lives of some, but because they never acknowledged the truth of what He said, a relationship was never formed. Even hypocrisy is not a deal breaker for Jesus, good news for all of us because it resides in every heart to some degree, but Jesus had the deepest relationships with those who followed Him with honesty.

They were not perfect, these Jesus-followers, nor were they honest 100% of the time, but they displayed a general desire and pursuit of it. A relationship with Jesus today is based on that same thing. Each of us must be willing to come to Him as we really are, frank about our current state and open to His perceptive evaluation of us. Without this, He cannot work in us what He longs to work, and the relationship will wither.

I told the mom how much I loved hearing her stories, which I did the first several times, and how I believed that the Lord had used her, which was also true. I told her that I hoped that, if hungry neighbors came to my house, I would be just like her and empty my fridge to feed them.

"But," I continued slowly, "I also long to hear what the Lord is doing in your life today. What is He doing? Maybe He's silent and you're angry that He won't speak. I want to hear about that. Maybe you're weary because of life, burdened by the things happening in your family.

"I want to hear about those things. Maybe you felt Him speak to you through His word. I want to hear about that. Maybe you're overwhelmed by your own weakness and rejection of the things the Lord has for you.

"I want to hear about that. I have heard about the fridge and God saw it and honors it and now it's time to move on to new things. If it was a crazy day, just tell me you didn't read your Bible, you might be surprised to hear that I didn't either and we can open that huge one right there on the table to read it together.

"Did you read yesterday, last week, last month? Is there any verse or truth from His word that He is using to rearrange your life? If not, it's time to reexamine. Let's go back together. He is waiting to work, to rebuild.

"Do you want that? I do. For me and for you, but it cannot happen if we only talk about stories from the past. I feel like I don't know what's happening in your life now. When I come next time would it be okay if we talked about Him and what's going on in the present?"

It felt like I was putting myself out there big time as I voiced what I was really thinking. But as I spoke, I knew that the Lord was working through me. It was me, but a different kind of me; a better kind. Have you had those moments? I'm sure you have.

You know that it's not you. I was bold and direct, but my harshness had been softened by genuine concern and the truth had been coated, saturated in grace, something that only the Spirit working in me could accomplish.

NOT SO DIFFERENT

I left that day in perfect peace. I had tried to do what the Lord had led me to do: even if it wasn't a perfect conversation and even if I didn't say all the right things. I had tried to be faithful to the Voice that had prompted me and I had shown true love to the person next to me. While those things amazed me, I was even more amazed that I had seen Him use a part of me that I thought was useless.

I thought that shutting my mouth was the answer to my harsh words, but He didn't agree. He wanted to make straight that which was crooked and return it to use. That's why He had long ago begun the work of revealing the problem that I was not a gentle dove. This was the culmination of years of underlying work in my heart.

The patience with which the Spirit works in the depths of who we are is mind boggling. I had given up on myself and resigned to shut that part of myself down. I didn't think change was possible. God knew better.

He can speak light into any unformed void in the world or in our hearts and that light sets the stage for new life. It might take a long time for the new life to have enough roots to grow and blossom, but it will.

Every one of us has rebuilding and renovating taking place under the surface, at least those of us who are sick of living in decay and rust.

I was trying to follow the Voice where it led that day. Interestingly, it led straight to the part of me that was being rebuilt. And that place was exactly the same one that the Voice was calling the mom to. She and I aren't that different.

There are parts of each of us that could use a revamp and it's always the same plumb line that starts the process. You see, I was not the plumb line—I just happened to be asked to hold it. In that moment, I was called in that way, to assist Him in a renovation.

Sometimes we are the ones holding the line. That takes humility, knowing that the same decay that caused the damage in others also resides in us. Other times, the line is held up to us by another. That also takes humility because then we must choose to be truthful about our actual state. I once heard humility defined as being who you really are. This includes the good and the bad; all of who I am.

Our true self is not an easy person to face, but when we confront it, we will be rewarded with genuine friendship first from the Friend of all friends and also by others who value truth and openness. It's the light shed by truth that sets the stage for new life of all kinds. Usually the light is turned on by a genuine friend.

THE WAIT

After leaving that day, I was so at peace that I just waited. I neither demanded a response from the mom nor was I anxiously checking my phone for a text from her.

In the same way, Jesus waits for each of us to respond without anxiety or pressure because He is in no hurry. He is also fully aware of the enormous amount of time it takes for real change to be worked through our minds, hearts, and souls.

Unfortunately, the mom responded with silence. Never again were we invited to sit in that living room. Friendships that could have been were not because the foundation refused to be laid. In some sense it's sad, but in another sense I am still waiting. If she were to change her mind and call me up, I would answer just like Jesus answers every time we change our minds and pursue Him.

Before you start getting the idea that I think I'm Jesus, let me take this moment to segue into our next story: a story that finds me on the opposite side. It finds me the hypocrite and I'm the one who almost missed out not because I was living in the past, but because I thought I knew and I didn't have a clue.

Things Worth Remembering

- Listen and ask questions if something doesn't make sense
- Boldly obey the prompts of the Spirit
- No honesty=no relationship
- No waste, 100% recycled is God's way

Kragujevac, Serbia

The city where it all
started

Chapter 7:

A POEM BY THE SEA

The most beautiful brown to match
the leaves
She's gleaming in the sun.

An entire chocolate bar? I remember thinking. *They do make little kid-sized ones, you know. Oh great, now he's crying because he can't eat the whole thing right now. Of course he can't, he's only one. Of all the gifts.*

More crying interrupted my thoughts. I'm not sure why that particular chocolate bar bothered me so much. Tadija, that screaming one-year-old, my son, got chocolate bars all the time; big, adult-sized chocolate bars. It's a part of the culture we live in. People love getting gifts for children. If someone comes over to our home, even if it's just for coffee, they will bring him a treat and maybe even a little toy. We should have had a drawer full of chocolate bars by his first birthday, but instead, Danny and I just ate them after he went to bed. I love that people here always think of children, but the huge chocolate bars I could do without, if I'm being honest.

It might be because chocolate does something to my little angel. It turns him into a raving addict demanding more and more until there is none left. Then, he turns into a ball of emotions because the candy is gone. In an attempt to avoid the drama, I hide the chocolate as soon as its shiny wrapper is spotted by my eagle-eye.

Sometimes, though, a bar will slip by unnoticed and that is what happened that Sunday morning. We were at church where I put this unrealistic pressure on my son to magically leave all selfishness at the door. Well, he clearly didn't get the memo. As he screamed for one more piece, his face scrunched into fit mode and my anxiety skyrocketed.

Maybe it was a stressful morning. Maybe I was just grouchy. Or maybe deeper things were coming to the surface. No matter the reason, I was thinking, *who started the chocolate*

tradition anyway? Can they please come and babysit my human
ball of emotion because I am done.

The current giver of chocolate sat seemingly
unconcerned feeding my addict more and more, which is also
common. When it comes to children and sweets there are
usually no limits.

What an inappropriate gift, I thought again. I thought I
knew better and I was also projecting my frustration on the
nearest unfortunate victim. After church, we headed home.
I hope that chocolate doesn't ruin his nap. I knew lunch was
already ruined, but held out hope for the nap. Sleep came
easy to that little chocolate-intoxicated child.

As I sat on the couch, I was still irritated about the
chocolate. I couldn't let it go. I felt completely justified in my
assumptions about its giver. What I was about to learn would
not only silence my internal bickering, but would be that
plumb line again. This time held up to me.

LISTENING CHANGES ALL

The lady sitting across from me, the giant chocolate bar
provider, wasn't a stranger. She had come over and been to
church several times, but this was the first time she had come
alone. She lived in another city and was part of a small home
group that Danny had visited for over a year, so he knew her
better than I did. My lack of knowledge was about to become
painfully obvious.

I made coffee and put out cookies and Danny started
asking questions. It was easier to talk with her now that she
came alone because her mom had done most of the talking

when they had come together. It took more time than usual for our conversation because she had to write down all of her answers on a piece of paper for us to read. A rare sickness had damaged her vocal cords as a toddler, leaving her unable to speak.

"Thank you for having me over," she wrote.

"Of course, anytime," Danny replied.

"No you don't understand, thank you" she continued. "Thank you for letting me come over to play with Tadija."

Tadija was now sleeping in his room, but the toy she had pulled out of her bag for him upon arrival was still sitting on the coffee table. He loved playing with her, even when there was no chocolate or toy involved, something I had noticed in spite of my frustration.

"You're welcome," he answered again.

"No, you don't understand, thank you for letting me be close to him and touch him."

Clearly we were not getting the significance of what she was saying, so she continued to write.

"Shortly after my first cousin once removed was born, Mom and I went to visit him. We took a bus several hours just to see him. I love kids and couldn't wait to hold him. When we finally arrived, my aunt came out and said that my mom was welcome to come in, but I was asked to wait outside. They didn't want me near the baby."

I stared at the slim, unimposing lady sitting on our couch, incredulous.

"They thought maybe I was cursed and that is why I got sick and became mute. They didn't want the curse to affect their baby. That or maybe someone in my family sinned and my muteness was a punishment from God. Either way, I was to wait outside."

As horrifying as it was, her story didn't surprise me since I had heard similar ones before. At this point, I am forced to stop and make something clear. Entering into another culture with appreciation and a willingness to assimilate is not the same thing as embracing every aspect of that culture. I love living where I live and I could talk a long time about the things I love, but loving is not always agreeing.

Every culture carries in it the brokenness that results from sin and evil. The culture I currently live in has such a strong undercurrent of shame that it hides special needs and abuse. It is not uncommon for special needs to be seen as a curse or worse: divine punishment for sin.

This kind of thinking is evil and I want nothing to do with it. It isn't true and I will never accept it no matter how long I live here. The shame that silences the abused is also evil and I will fight against it as long as I live. Loving a culture and its people is not the same as turning a blind eye to the evils therein. Fully entering in forces your eyes open as you find yourself so close to it all. Either I live in reality with all its brokenness and evil, or I separate myself entirely and create my own.

I choose to live in it, but sometimes there are moments when I hate the reality I find myself in. Reading those words that day was one of those moments.

"You see, now it doesn't matter because I get to come and play with Tadija. Thank you so much for letting me play with him. I just love watching him and being close to him."

I exhaled slowly, that chocolate bar was the overflow of a

love for and delight in my son. No one had ever told me that they loved to come and watch him play or that they loved just being in the same room as him. I knew that Tadija felt that love because he was drawn to her and loved her back with all the intensity toddler-love can possess.

In my pride, I had almost rejected that love and intercepted that delight. I had almost been just like those cousins. Of course not totally—I never would have kept Tadija from her simply because she could not speak. But I had assumed that her heart-gift was inappropriate. I had assumed that I knew better.

One of my dearest friends had the spunkiest grandma and this wise woman would always say, "Now you know what you do when you assume? You make an ass out of 'u' and 'me'." That is exactly what I felt like. That initial perception that I had about her was completely wrong.

I had made a huge false assumption. Her chocolate bar was absolutely appropriate because it was the overflow of pure love. It might have been inconvenient since Tadija always demanded the entire thing, but it was an extension of her delight in him. I had completely missed out on that because of my pride. I thought I knew, but I hadn't had a clue.

It's worth our time to check our first impressions. Sometimes they are right on and sometimes they are completely wrong. The truth and I were not even in the same country, but sitting in a living room asking questions saved me from being stuck in my wrongness. Maybe it doesn't matter so much whose living room it is, ours or theirs, but more that we are there, sitting together asking questions, getting closer to the truth.

A SPECIAL FRIENDSHIP

This lady still comes to our house and I now anticipate her visits, and yes, she is usually holding a big bar of chocolate. Tadija is more excited than I am, but just barely. I enjoy being in her company. I love it when she walks through the door and Tadija yells, "Mama, Kiki is here!" A smile spreads across her face as she hears those words and off they go to play together in Tadija's room.

I love that Tadija gets to know such a special lady: that I get to know such a special lady. And I keep reminding myself that I almost didn't get that chance because that Sunday morning is a past that's not worth repeating. Better to remember and learn than to forget and repeat my foolishness.

I almost robbed my entire family of a friend. No, more than a friend, of a sister and an aunt. I almost robbed us of community with one of the most generous spirits I know. Our false assumptions have power. We must check them. It's worth stopping to ask questions. You might just discover a new friend. You might add a new member to your family.

Kiki's friendship not only enriches my and Danny's lives but also the life of our son. He doesn't even realize what a privilege it is to receive such pure love or how cool it is to know a secret language with your hands. He will not remember the time that Kiki took us to the sea but he will be able to relive parts of it because she gave him a special gift.

It's a poem she wrote for him about our 9 days together. Sharing the poem in its entirety would only bring confusion because the special places and moments were shared by just us, but I would like to give you a taste of what it contains. Here is a section of what she wrote:

"I want you to know, Tadija, what a big thing you did in my life by coming to the sea with me, your mom, and your dad. You opened a door in me that no one had before, some didn't even try. Your mom and dad will explain to you what I mean by a 'door'. I'm not talking about a door to a house or a building. You brought joy into my life, the reason I'm alive, and you did it by running in the sand, holding my hand as we walked, and asking all kinds of questions.

I want you to keep this poem. Since I consider your mom a sister and your dad a brother that means I consider myself your aunt. I want you to know that I love you as an aunt. You are a part of me. Don't be afraid to tell me anything, to ask me for or about anything. I am here, ready to laugh with you or when necessary to wipe away your tears.

What I have written in this poem is the truth, written from my heart. It's not imagined or exaggerated.

Thank the Lord that He sent Tadija to this world!

Thank you Danny and Wendy for bringing him into this world!

Thank you Tadija for existing and for being you!"

Now you see what my assumptions almost lost us all. You understand the heart behind that chocolate bar and now you agree I was terribly wrong. It's a gift not to be trapped in our wrongness. We can step right out of it if we choose to move into the truth. It's that simple. Better to be willing to be wrong and to invite change instead of choosing to stay the same and rob yourself of friendships like Kiki's. If you have children, I think they would love to have an aunt like her and I think your heart longs for someone to love your children just for being them. No performance needed. No comparing, just delight in their existence.

Delight might be hidden behind your wrong assumptions. Admitting that and readjusting your perspective might introduce you to a Kiki of your own, opening a torrent of joy from them and for them. Allow yourself to admit you were wrong and to be corrected. Or, keep assuming and remain a donkey forever.

Things Worth Remembering

- *First impressions are real*
- *Background information is vital*
- *Step out of wrong assumptions*
- *Better yet, don't assume!*

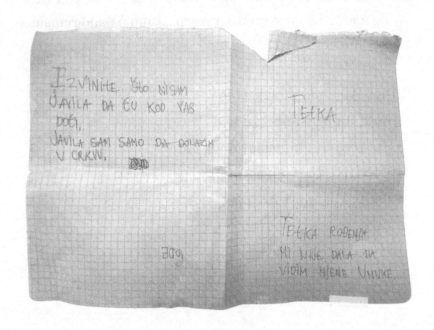

Notes from Kiki

Kiki and Tadija headed
down to the beach

Chapter 8:

CIGARETTE BUTTS IN THE MATERNITY WARD

It's just a deer, but not to me
She's a jewel of the woods.

Going on little adventures is a regular part of our family time. We love going into the woods, picking a new path each time and following where it leads. One day, we were exploring a new path and as we came around a bend, I noticed an apple on the ground. *Someone must have been here cutting wood and dropped their apple,* I thought. Then I saw another and another and another. The ground in front of me was covered with apples. I called my family to stop with me and solve the mystery of where the apples came from.

Standing in the middle of them, I looked up and sure enough, I was under a huge apple tree. It was definitely ugly, with broken branches and a leaning trunk, but at that moment it was a special surprise. For me, that made it beautiful, like a hidden treasure. The apples were sweet and tart, some of the best apples I have ever had. I can't be sure if it was the quality of the apples or the surprise of finding them that made them so enjoyable. Either way, we headed home with pockets stuffed full of apples and a memory to revisit together.

The adventure that is about to be revisited is also filled with forest apples, unexpected treasures that can refresh a thirsty mouth with fresh juice or remind a lonely soul that someone walked that path before. Apple trees grow from apple seeds, either dropped or planted there by someone who walked that path long before the trees took root. Even the fact that a path exists means that someone made it, carving it out of the surrounding forest.

We walk hundreds of different paths in our lifetimes and, if we are paying attention, each has treasure scattered along the way. The adventure I want to talk about in this chapter led to the greatest treasure I have ever received and forest apples planted by One who went before me: nurtured and grown by my Path Maker.

It all started with a little line and that landed me in the waiting room at the doctor's office. They say that the line doesn't lie, but a doctor's visit would confirm it. I waited anxiously. Doctor's appointments are never my idea of a good time. The good thing about waiting was that it gave time for my mind to review all of the vocabulary that I would need to successfully communicate with the doctor.

Years of living and doing life in a second language has trained my brain for this kind of thing. My mind preps my mouth as I enter the grocery store, or the post office, or a friend's house, mentally collecting the appropriate list of words and phrases I need. I had to learn some new ones for this visit, though, so my mind was working harder than usual.

They called my name. I understood that. It was a good start: don't underestimate the power of a good start. I walked back into the examination room and was met by a middle-aged woman.

She started by asking politely about my name, a routine I have gotten used to. Her face said, "Why do you have such a weird name?" but her mouth said, "Vendi, what an unusual name."

I gave my standard response, one I knew wasn't likely to earn any further questioning. "I'm not from here, my husband is Serbian."

She smiled and nodded, this was no exception.

Oh good, she's nice. I breathed a little easier, but my brain was still on high alert.

"So, did you bring a condom?" She continued.

Alarm bells. My ears must be paying a sick trick on my brain. "Excuse me?" I said. My mind sifted through all the words I knew, trying to find one that sounded like condom but made more sense. *Mondom, dondom, stondom.* Meaningless rhyming words were all I came up with.

"Did you bring a condom?" she repeated.

Ok, I definitely understand the word, but still not the question. I wanted to answer, "Obviously not, that's why I am here," but all that came out was, "No I didn't. Was I supposed to?"

"Ok then we will try with a linear probe. How far along are you?"

"About 7 weeks I think." I lay down on the table and proceeded to have one of the most amazing experiences of my life. I honestly couldn't make out the baby on the screen. There was a blob mixed into a blur. There was a clear disconnect in my brain as I looked at the screen. *That doesn't look like a baby.* But hearing that little heart beat, that was magical. In an instant, I was overwhelmed with the knowledge that I was now a mother.

That little heartbeat began my journey down a new path: one previously unknown. Sometimes I felt nervous. Other times I was downright terrified. I

was never alone, though, and, in spite of this adventure being on an unfamiliar path, it was–as I would see–well prepared and filled with treasure.

PREPARATION FOR MOTHERHOOD

The first question to answer after the heartbeat confirmed that line was right was "Where will we have the baby?" We had several options, but decided on the local hospital. There is a saying here, "Nothing gets done without a connection," and so knowing one of the head pediatricians who worked in the birthing wing of the hospital was crucial. The doctor who would follow my pregnancy would be secured through her recommendation. All extra tests would get done because of my connection with her. She would be there for the birth even if it was not her shift.

Things here change if you have connections: people are a little more patient and you are treated with more care. Having such a significant connection was as if Someone had gone before me and removed not just one but all the logs from my path making it so much easier to navigate and follow.

I did everything that I could to prepare for giving birth in a foreign hospital. I was also preparing for being a mom by reading and talking to friends, but somehow the actual birth was for me more intimidating. I was already fluent in the language, but hospitals, babies, and pregnancy brought with them a whole new set of vocabulary and mentality. As my little boy grew in my belly, so did my knowledge of hospital terms, nursing words, and general baby vocabulary. Even the word for "push" is different in this language when it is the pushing involved in giving birth. A good fact to know.

I joined "The School for Pregnant Ladies," as it was called, and sat in each class with my notebook and pen. It looked like I was getting ready for some giant final exam, but mostly I was just writing down words and phrases I didn't know. At home, I would look up all the words, try to memorize them, and study all the brochures I had been given. I figured as long as I understood the 'birth lingo' I would be fine. I had given up trying to speak with perfect grammar years ago.

As a part of our class, we went to a gym twice a week and did exercises together to ready our bodies to squeeze out little humans. Those times were my favorite as we all laughed and peed our pants together, rolling around on the floor, feeling like a pod of beached whales. We lay on our backs and practiced the three stages of labor followed by the corresponding breathing techniques. All of us were in our 8th month of pregnancy. We were in it together, another treasure. The school lasted a month and shortly after that notifications began arriving in our group chat accompanied by pictures of newborns.

D-DAY

One July 11th, it was my turn. I was adamant not to have my baby steal my birthday, but he inherited my determination and made his entry on that date anyway. It was a relatively quick delivery; I was only in the hospital for 2 hours after I had labored at home with my pediatrician on the phone. She wanted me to wait as long as possible because she said once I went in to the hospital I would have to labor in bed, unable to walk around. She had me wait until my contractions were 5 minutes apart and then, we zipped away to the hospital, which was 10 minutes away.

Our pediatrician friend was waiting for me there and

proceeded to sit next to me the entire 2 hours of my time in the delivery room, as Danny was not allowed to join me. Husbands are never allowed in, so I was prepared for this, but seeing a familiar face was more comforting than I had anticipated. She also snuck a mutual friend in, and hearing that friend's voice from the side of the room telling me I was doing great was calming and stabilizing, like the taste of forest apples after a long hike.

Tadija was broad-shouldered, which they already knew from my ultrasounds and so the gynecologist decided an episiotomy was the safest option. He did his job with confidence and explained everything as he went, reassuring me that everything was going well. Explanations are usually not given to patients, so I took that as an extra grace: a treasure.

Tadija came out screaming and as the pediatrician handed him over to me, I could hear my friend from the corner say, "You did it, Wendy."

I counted all his fingers. Ten. He was a perfect, healthy little boy. I held him for a couple of minutes and then they took him to be examined more closely. The doctor and nurses were hurrying to the next room to deliver another baby. One nurse was left with me. She turned around, looked at me, and then quickly left the room. Suddenly, the doctor and the other nurse rushed back in, telling my friend she had to leave. I had no idea what was going on. The doctor was very calm and told me that I had internal tearing and needed stitches immediately. Unfortunately, he could not give me anesthesia, but would be as fast and gentle as possible.

It wasn't until one of the nurses asked to use my tissues

that I became more aware of how dangerous the situation was. She pulled off one of her shoes and began wiping the blood off of it. My blood. The tearing had caused considerable bleeding.

I would later learn that that doctor was not only well respected and called to give seminars around the country, but was also the director of the entire Clinical Center at the time. Tadija was born at 10 pm and his shift ended at 12. The doctor working the next shift was nicknamed 'the butcher' because he was so rough and was infamous for giving good care only after having received an outrageous bribe. Again, my Path Maker had been at work, clearing the thorns and danger from my path.

My spiritual family was also at work as they lifted us up through countless prayers. I will never be able to communicate how much those prayers meant to me and what a privilege it was to experience their answers. Each detail of my path was crafted by the Path Maker. He did not remove all pain and darkness, those things will always be on our paths, but I could clearly see that He had made a way for me to walk in.

A ROOM WITH SHADOWS AND LAUGHTER

Darkness did abide in the days following Tadija's birth, in ways that many new mothers have experienced. I was so sore the day after delivering that I couldn't walk. I didn't realize that I was responsible to give and administer pain medication to myself. I didn't want to see or talk to anyone, even my husband. Tadija was shown to Danny through the glass in the hallway, but I didn't leave my room. I couldn't go to the bathroom myself and the nurse had to shower me. I would rather forget those memories.

I had such a strong flow of milk at once that my ducts became completely clogged. Two nurses spent countless hours massaging them to get the milk flowing. During the day, in the middle of the night, it didn't matter, they were there one on each side trying to unclog the ducts. There were no heating pads in the hospital to assist in this, so a hot water bottle was the next best thing—a literal plastic 2-liter bottle filled with hot water. The warmth soothed my swollen, bruised breasts, but only during the day. After 10 pm, there was no hot water until the next morning. When I asked about it, they led me to their staff kitchen to the one faucet on the entire floor that had hot water at night.

"Come and get fresh, hot water whenever you need to," the nurses said.

They even snuck fresh cabbage leaves into the hospital to put on my breasts as I slept.

Slowly the warmth, massages, cabbage, and Tadija nursing unclogged my ducts and the milk started flowing. It would take a week or so for them to be completely unclogged, but thankfully, it didn't get worse, mostly because of the care I received by the nurses. I was never alone in those dark few days. It was especially that first night that I didn't feel alone, which is a miracle because Tadija was not with me and so I was the only person in the room. Tadija had high blood sugar and so they were giving him an infusion of some sort just to be safe. I was physically alone for a couple of hours, but rarely have I felt the presence of the Lord in such a powerful way.

He was right there. The darkness was too and it pressed against my soul, but His presence never abandoned me to it.

One of my prayers before giving birth was to be in a room with a woman who had given birth to a second or third child, someone already familiar with the ins and outs of the hospital. The Path Maker gave me two of them—and a window seat! My bed was closest to the window, which is a big deal when there is no air conditioning and it's July in the Balkans. The lady next to me had her second son a couple of hours after me and the one in the bed by the door had hers a couple of hours after her. Both knew exactly what was expected and I relied on them heavily.

One morning I was eating breakfast at the little table in the corner when one whisper-yelled, "What are you doing? Get in bed."

I looked confused, but obeyed and slowly climbed onto my bed.

"Cover your legs quickly, they're doing rounds."

I pulled the blanket up to my waist and waited, imitating her and the lady between us; hands folded, eyes fixed straight ahead, back straight. In walked the head doctor and his entourage. He told each member of his posse the details of our individual cases.

"She has blocked milk ducts we need to keep an eye on that." He waved his hand at me.

"She is having trouble getting the baby to latch on." He gestured to my neighbor.

"She's doing great." His pen pointed to the third lady and with that they all left.

We all exhaled before the lady who was doing great got

up and explained, "When the doctor comes through to do his rounds every morning at 8:30, you have to be in bed with your covers on."

Good to know, I thought.

She also helped me with many other dos and don'ts that I have now forgotten. The middle lady was not as positive, but vital for a different reason: she made us laugh. One day she came back into the room reeking of cigarette smoke. She quickly sprayed perfume all over herself, creating a nauseating combination of stink. The other mom in the room and I burst out laughing.

"What?" She asked. "Do you think they will still be able to tell that I was smoking? I just can't quit."

We laughed even harder.

"I hid the evidence. Can you still smell the smoke?"

We laughed until our stitches hurt. You could smell everything in there, thanks to the lack of ventilation, but she was convinced she had covered her tracks. Later, when I went to take a shower, I burst out laughing again. There, shoved in the cracks between several of the chipped bathroom tiles, were her cigarette butts, partially sticking out.

Laughter became like a medicine for us and we got another dose when a nurse walked into the room and looked at each of us, paused and said, "Who the heck is Vendoo Loon?"

"That's me." I was still laughing. "It's a typo on my health insurance card. My name is Vendi Lin." (There are no Ws or Ys in Serbian.)

This time the nurse laughed, "And this whole time I was looking for a Chinese lady."

We laughed when family members of the lady closest to the door snuck food in for her. She sat on her bed and unwrapped the large kitchen towel revealing a birthday cake and huge pieces of roasted pork. With wide eyes she stared at the feast in front of her. "How am I supposed to eat all this? What were they thinking?"

The nurse, however, did not laugh when she caught her munching on the meat, yelling about ants, which sent us into another fit of laughter because ants would have plenty to find even if her meat hadn't appeared.

We laughed when a nurse turned the TV on and then informed us that there was only one remote control for the entire floor to share and it had been lost. When we realized that we were all too short to reach up and change the channel manually, the reality show playing acted as our background music for the next day and night. When we thought our brains would turn to mush and just wanted some peace and quiet a lady in the room next to us agreed to come and turn the TV off. She was just tall enough. All of these are little details and many may seem insignificant, but not to me. I see them as evidence of help and design. They are my forest apples. As I revisit these memories, I see how laughter drew out the sting of pain and struggle, not completely but just enough.

These two ladies kept an eye on Tadija while I showered or went to the bathroom and I did the same for them. We shared snacks, cooling spray, and stories. When the fourth day came and it was time for Tadija and me to leave the hospital, we laughed and cried and hugged: special moments along the path that I replay often in my mind.

TREASURE ALONG A PATH REVISITED

I walked out the door of the maternity ward and hugged Danny for the first time since we had become parents. We changed Tadija from the clothes the hospital provided into his first little outfit, which barley fit over his chunky legs. Then we carefully secured him in his car seat. We walked down the stairs and out the doors into the July sun. I wanted to run to the car to get home faster, but walking was all my body would allow. With Tadija safely buckled in the back seat we headed home to begin our new life together. This time, three of us instead of two.

It took time before I was ready to revisit those first few dark days and time for me to process how hard Danny's side of the story had been during that time. He had been bed-ridden by back pain off and on for 6 months before Tadija was born. He broke out in shingles the day we arrived home from the hospital because of the stress surrounding the birth. Worst of all, he had lost his dad suddenly 2 months before Tadija arrived. There was a lot of stress, sadness, joy, and exhaustion all living in the same space at the same time. It took a long time for us to find a new normal and talk through it all, but as we did this we also uncovered the treasures that were along the path.

Did you see it as you walked my path with me? I hope you felt the pain and sensed the darkness because they were real, but even more than that I hope you saw the light. Each skilled person in the right place at the right time to care for me and for Tadija: treasure. Laughter and friends: great treasures. Kindness: more treasure. And of course, new life: the greatest of treasures.

As I walk this path again in my mind, memory has allowed me to slowly turn over each stone and stoop to brush away the leaves and uncover treasures that I had missed before. Revisiting old paths can do that: unearth treasure overlooked. But it's the Path Maker who continues to awe me the most. I see anew that One went before me, clearing the way, making it safe and walkable. Not easy, manageable. I remember afresh the One who was right beside me walking the path with me, even the parts that were hidden in the shadows. I understand that One went behind me, protecting me and the baby as we walked. My trail blazer, my companion and my rear guard, He truly is the perfect Guide, going before us, staying with us and watching us from behind.

Only He can be all three at once. Only He can do it with perfect knowledge and endless compassion. We do not walk our paths alone and we can trust the Voice that calls to us and says, "I am your friend...I've been working on your path, do you want to see it? If you follow it carefully, you will find new treasures, but it won't be an easy journey. Go ahead; here I am right beside you. Let's go, discover my gifts of love for you."

Things Worth Remembering

- *Paths unknown to us have been prepared by the Path Maker*
- *If it is dark and hard, that is ok*
- *Your Guide is the best of the best*

- The fellowship with your Guide along the way is precious
- Look for the treasures along the way

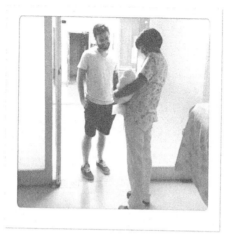

Danny meeting Tadija for
the first time

The start of a new adventure—
Motherhood

Chapter 9

SCRIBBLES

A trail, oh wow I see it now.
I'm not as lost as I thought.

Not all treasure is so obvious to identify. Sometimes the treasure is a supernatural revelation that something has gone wrong. Things in our world are constantly going awry. The toilets start leaking, the roads get potholes, and our favorite shirts get stained. We live in a constant state of dystopia and our inner worlds are no different. We are in constant need of re-centering. I am in constant need of re-centering my inner world, especially my desires.

I start out great, right in the middle of the path, desiring something good and God-breathed. But, over time I slowly veer and, because I'm not paying attention, end up lost in the woods, no path in sight.

The 'center' of the path in my next story, was a strong desire to become fluent in the language that was spoken in my new home. Actually, the center was not even the desire to speak, but the reason for speaking. I wanted to be able to talk about deep spiritual things with my neighbors in their heart language. I longed to interact with their hearts as well as their minds to enter into their world in order to point them to the One who entered so perfectly into mine. This aspiration did not originate in my heart. It was something that the Lord had worked into me, another transplanted desire. It started out as a crushing burden to go to a certain people group and then a crushing burden to speak using the words that they already knew and held so dear.

This new language would be the third language, other than High School French, that I would attempt to learn. As you have already seen, standing in a room not understanding one word being spoken, was not a new experience to me, but this venture would become my longest pursuit of a language and the only one to end in fluency. Remember the Special Needs Club? That was at the beginning of this journey toward making sense of this new language. Think back to my confusion and sense of uselessness. Remember? Ok then we're ready to continue.

THE JOURNEY TOWARD FLUENCY

Learning a language is embarrassing and because of past experience, I understood in part the monumental task before me. The grammar of this new language is complex and just as foreign as the letters themselves. There are two alphabets, Latin and Cyrillic, and the use of vowels is optional. "R" acts as a vowel, so they are not exactly absent, but to my foreign tongue they might as well be because pronouncing words like *smrt* require a complete realignment of every one of my facial muscles. Because of the difficulty I was having pronouncing such words, I would pick one and say it out loud over and over again until I could enunciate it.

This word, *smrt*, was in the hot seat and I was practicing it one day as I walked down the street. I was not being obnoxious or loud, just muttering it to myself. I was determined for it to roll off my tongue with ease. After a while, I became aware that almost every person passing me was giving me a confused, slightly concerned look. I figured I just looked extra foreign that day and continued on my merry way, but as the looks continued I began to get self-conscious. What did I do this time to stamp myself, "imported"? I was racking my brain as I continued my self-imposed language lesson, "*smrt, smrt, smrt,*" I mumbled. It was not until I got home that

I realized why everyone was so concerned for me. I would be concerned too if I passed a person on the street saying, "death, death, death." The real lesson that day was, be careful which words you practice out loud in public. Death is not a good word to mutter over and over again in the city center.

It took me a couple of years to move from mumbling one word over and over again to talking in full sentences. As I began talking, the Lord brought very patient friends into my life and I continued to progress. It is impossible to list all of the people who played a part in this process, there are too many, but I would like to stop and reiterate the important role they played. A couple of friends patiently listened to me and corrected only my major mistakes; this grew my confidence. A group of people who met weekly in our home let me fumble my way through a prayer request, and sometimes a prayer itself giving me invaluable practice. The many who prayed for me here and abroad lifted my spirits when I wanted to give up, which was often.

Years of learning led to more words in my brain, friendships built in that language and the assurance that it was actually possible to become fluent. One day, I would be able to share about the hope within me using those vowelless words and that day was coming soon.

THE VEER

When Danny and I moved to our current home, I was the only foreigner that I knew in the entire city. This gave me a unique opportunity to learn the language through complete immersion. The only time I spoke English was at home with

Danny, teaching an English lesson or talking on the phone to family. It was intense and it worked. I was understanding more and being understood better. Win, win. Then, over a period of a few years, several other English-speaking families moved to the city and became a part of our church. It was a new dynamic and it did something to my inner world. It started a veer.

I did not realize it at the time, but a sick game of 'who speaks the best' started in my heart. I began to strive to be the best, not in order to serve those around me, but in order to beat them. Pride, selfish ambition and unhealthy competition fueled me along. I was going to be better than any other foreigner at speaking this new language. That is the steam train I was on and thank God that it crashed.

I still remember exactly where I was and who I was talking to when it happened. It was another couch, but not in a living room. Sun was streaming through the windows of the space we rented for church services and other events. It was a beautiful day. I was talking to a lady about nothing in particular when she casually said, "You speak our language better than any other foreigner I know."

We knew the same foreigners. I had reached my goal. I should have been ecstatic, but all I wanted to do was throw up. A physical sensation of nausea shot through my entire body the moment her words reached my ears. The truth is I had not even admitted to myself that my once good and pure motive had been covered over by another. I felt defeated and grieved. The parasite of comparison had silently grown within me.

Who will be the greatest? I was just as determined to reach

the top as the disciples had been 2,000 years ago and just like then, that kind of greatest has no place in Jesus's kingdom now. It will be confronted. To be better than everyone else wasn't my initial goal, but in that moment I realized that it had become my chief desire and that was a bitter revelation. I didn't want to admit it, but I had to. The nausea told all.

Wormwood is a bitter plant, but a bitter plant with healing power. Ingesting its bitterness can help restore that which in the body has gone awry, it can restore health but it must be ingested. Smelling it is not enough. Touching it is not enough. It must be swallowed, fully absorbed. Hearing that statement that day, presented me with a choice.

The truth behind the words was like bitter wormwood held up to me. What would I do with it? Ingest its bitterness, and hope that there would be some health benefit or turn up my nose and walk away? There have been plenty of times that I have done the latter, but this time was different. Maybe it was the grief in my spirit that slowed me down enough to examine the medicinal properties of the bitter. Maybe I recognized the Voice behind the spoken words, I'm not sure. But what I did know was that I was genuinely saddened by what exploded from my heart. I had become someone that I didn't want to be. Those foreigners were my friends and I knew the agony of their language endeavors and here I was pushing them down so that I would appear to be a little taller.

SCRIBBLES FOR DAD

I was defeated by the mutation my goal of fluency had undergone. It used to be beautiful. In the beginning, I could proudly hold up my progress to my heavenly Dad and know that He was proud of my endeavors. I knew it wasn't an impressive feat, struggling to learn some new letters. It was equivalent to the scribbles of my 3-year-old, but I also knew that He loved to see those scribbly efforts just as much as I loved to see Tadija's. His scribbles are more than just lines on a page for me. They are a window into his world and when I am invited in, I jump at the opportunity.

"What does it look like, Mama?" He asks every time his marker stops swirling.

I squint and find somewhere to place an eyeball and tell him, "a dragon, of course."

"Yes." He giggles as he draws his next creation. "What does it look like, Mama?"

"Oh, that's definitely a car." I quickly add some wheels somewhere, my smile as big as his. He shows those drawings to me in complete freedom, no matter what they actually look like. He knows I will see something in them and bring it out by adding a couple of eyes or wheels or a tail maybe. He isn't embarrassed by what he made and invites me into his creative process. I love it.

My venture into an unknown language was not that different. It was as if I had a piece of paper and on it was my newfound knowledge. A scribble of Serbian. Face beaming, I held up my jumble of letters saying, "What does it look like, Dad?"

He added a couple of eyes and beamed, "a missionary of course."

I could feel His joy as He added those eyeballs. I sensed that He loved that I was trying something new and even more that I was sharing my efforts with Him.

Sitting on that couch, sick to my stomach was a different experience. I suddenly became ashamed of that scribble, my desire to be fluent. It had changed. It was as if I had smeared manure all over the page, covering up the original picture. I was suddenly afraid to show it to Dad.

What would His response be when I asked, "What does it look like, Dad?"

In my mind He would say, "Oh wow, that's stinky. This picture is ruined. I'll just take that and throw it away. You know, you really should have been more careful. Couldn't you at least smell it?"

My default is to hide every spoiled picture in between all the other pictures so my Dad doesn't see it. I act like it doesn't exist, only to pull it out when I'm alone to analyze it and find new ways to feel guilty about it. This time though, I tried something new.

I fought through my fear of disappointing and held up that mess to my Dad and said, "Look, Dad. I wanted to make a pretty picture for You but this is what I made instead. It's really ugly and it stinks."

I let the tears fill my eyes instead of stashing them away for the bathroom. I allowed myself to feel sad about what I had learned about myself. I even went as far as to admit that being better than everyone else was my desire, revealing a genuine part of me. It was a part of who I was, but a part that I didn't want anymore. I didn't even want to analyze it. I yearned to go back to learning in order to share stories: in order to share life. So I gave that picture to Dad and do you know what He did? He began to clean the stink. It's grace that

that lady said what she did. It stopped me and gave me the opportunity to say, "Dad, look at the mess I made. Look at the mess that I am."

How He reacted to my admission, both surprised and humbled me. He put me back in the middle of where I should have been all along. My sin is destructive and divisive and there is no excuse for it. Its presence, though, is no surprise to my Dad because He already smells the manure and has already put events and people in place to re-center me and to remove the stink.

He is waiting to take the mess I have made, the mess that I am. He gently washes my hands and gives me a new piece of paper. No guilt-trip. He knows that I get it. I see the lesson to be learned and He is not concerned with proving a point, but with recreating a heart. My scribbles are more than just performance for Him: efforts to be graded. They are a window into my heart and when invited, He jumps at the opportunity to take what is there and add His touch. It's sometimes an improvement like some eyes or wheels and it's sometimes a new sheet of paper.

He does not throw the old, stinky one away though. He is wise enough to know that there is power in remembering the stench, not to shame, but to enlighten. Looking back at that ruined scribble reminds me that I don't want to go back to that place again. I want to stay right in the middle of the path He has set before me. It prompts me to examine my desires often to see if they have morphed. Keeping that scribble also reminds me of His reaction to it. Next time I mess up and stink something up, if I remember, I will run to Him and tell Him everything and ask for help. He helped me before and

He will help me again and again and again. In the meantime, He waits for my next scribble. With my new fresh sheet of paper, I am once again free to move on and create something new: to try something new.

"What does it look like, Dad?" I'll ask.

He will chuckle, add some wheels and transform it into something beautiful: an outward expression of our relationship. The beauty isn't in the picture, but in the smiles of Father and child as they create together.

Things Worth Remembering

- Motives can warp and distort over time
- God reveals to free and restore
- Bravely give your heavenly Dad your mess
- He isn't surprised and is waiting to help

What does it look like, Mama?

БАС
БЕОГРАДСКА АУТОБУСКА СТАНИЦА

Аутобуска карта   N 0584105
1809 0755 6092-29063062

БЕОГРАД-   КРАГУЈЕВАЦ АС

Превозник АС КРАГУЈЕВАЦ
Датум   18.09.12   Цена   690,00
Време   08:00   Попуст
Перон   11   Ст. услугаIII   120,00
Кола   1   Резервац.   0,00
Седиште 25   Доб.осиг.ДУНАВ   20,00
                   Хум.Акције   17,00
                   Укупно дин.   847,00

My bus pass

Chapter 10:

ONE SKIP SHORT

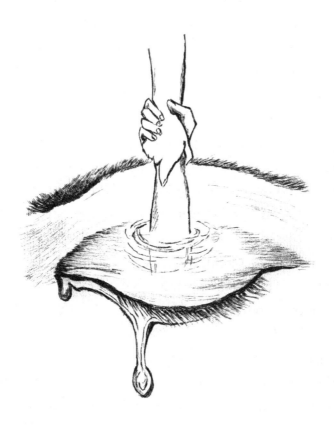

So there I sit in silence
The woods have finally won.

My fingers want to stop pounding the keys as I reach this part. Each letter must be typed slowly and takes extra effort. If I had it my way, I wouldn't write this chapter at all. I would avoid it, just like I wanted to avoid walking through the open gate of our next story. I would just skip this chapter and move to the next thing. That is something that I do, not only in my writing, but also in my life. I skim over the sad parts like a skipped rock along the surface of a lake, landing as far away from the feeling as possible. Heaven forbid I move one skip too short and land right in the middle of everything.

Even then, I pull out a safety raft, some robotic arms magically appear at the sides of my rock body and I paddle as fast and far away as robotically possible. I observe the lake, the surrounding trees, the reflection of the sun as I go, leaving no room for my mind to wander back to the sad place. Once at a safe distance, I do, do, do, and work, work, work. All in order to avoid just being. Usually this helps. Rarely do I find myself stuck one skip short. But what I did not realize was the cost of such frantic avoidance: the cost to myself and to those around me.

That cost is becoming painfully obvious to me, which adds another layer to the slowness of my typing. The cost of stopping the skip is: I sink. I settle at the bottom of the sadness and just sit there and my 'get up and get busy' self begins to squirm. I want to fix the sadness away. I want to inspire it into happiness. I want to tape over it with a Bible verse about hope and life plans. I want to change it.

There is just one problem. Sometimes, oftentimes, life really is sad. I mean devastatingly sad. And when I cover over the sadness and race to the happy things, I cover over a significant part of my life. Even worse, I cover over pieces of the lives of those next to me if it is *their* sadness I'm skipping over. That robs me and my friendships of depth. Skipping across the surface skips the deep that is explored only when I am willing to sink.

Sadness entered my life with a crash when my Father was tragically killed in a plane accident when I was just six years old. I am no stranger to sad things, but it has taken me my whole life to process that period, and that intense, other-worldly sadness and I have kept company. I can be sure that what I felt was sadness because I spent many nights screaming myself to sleep. It was my way of saying "This isn't fair. Why us? This isn't the way things should be." Those thoughts and the millions of other ones were combined with hurts that a child can't articulate with words.

It was my heart groaning, but I didn't realize how those groanings affected other areas of my life. Surprisingly, I was not a sad or depressed child in general. I was almost always happy and full of joy. Looking back, I consider my childhood to be a happy one. Even though there was tragedy, it did not define my younger years. I sometimes called to remembrance the sadness I felt then, but until recently I would never really sit in it.

I don't know if it was because of my early plunge into sad, or if it is part of my personality or something else, but over the years I slowly developed the philosophy that life is tragic enough without me sitting around thinking about said sadness. Now, I question the wisdom in such an attitude. A recent plunge to the bottom of the lake, the deepest lake I have ever known, has given me time to think, search, and wrestle with the pain sadness brings. It has given me the opportunity to lament.

THE OPEN GATE

Stop. Reflect. Push into the inconvenience of the stillness and just be. Allow the thoughts to come to the surface—you know—the ones you've been pushing aside, burying under busyness. Allow your muscles to relax, listen to your body. Breathe. The pen can only move so fast. Slow your racing mind. Invite the Spirit into the mess of your soul. Listen.

It is one thing to enter into the pain and darkness (could I add sadness?) of those around you, but it is quite another to be forced into your own personal darkness and have the door locked behind you. My heart beats faster. It's pitch black in every direction. "Am I alone? Who or what is locked in here with me? Will I ever get out?"

This is something that I wrote to myself in my journal during my time at the bottom of the lake. I had no idea that the feelings felt and written about would prepare me to bravely walk through the open gate of our next story.

The gate was open. It was never left open and I didn't like the eerie feeling inside me as I walked through it. I turned right, I walked up the stairs and through the door. Never in a million years could I have imagined that just as my friend held me as my son entered the world, I would hold her right after her son left it: prematurely left it when he took his own life. I hugged her, my grip almost too tight because hugging her was the only thing I could think to do. No words came, just tears and an ache from deep within.

That ache was given words a couple of days later at her son's funeral. The cold air crept under my jacket and the fog settled around the mass of black fabric on sunken bodies that surrounded the coffin. The big candle burned at the foot of it, but why? The life inside the box was already snuffed out.

I hated that candle. Candles belong in windows to keep the frost at bay as they guide home those who have wandered. They can do nothing to bring back a lost soul. Danny and I flowed with the multitude around the coffin to give our condolences to the mother and father. This is the same mother I had hugged and cried with 2 days prior, but we both still had tears left to cry.

The sadness tore even deeper into my heart as we approached them standing next to the corpse that just days before had held the spirit of their only son. Ironically, one could almost pretend away the pain were it not for the two of them. The casket was made of beautifully engraved wood. Polished to a shine and draped in spotless white lace. It was almost serene and it would have been easy to allow the beauty to beguile me. But as I walked around the casket, my eyes were met with the ashen white face of the mother and the clenched jaw of the father. What do you say when you can't even breathe? I hugged her, my grip definitely too tight this time, and then walked back to my place as others were waiting behind me to pay their respects.

I happened to be standing next to the aunt of the deceased.

I waited and all the tranquility that my mind had tried desperately to conjure up vanished as the mother flung her arms around that beautiful box. Her lips pressed against it and her tears dripped down the engraved flowers. Her moans vibrated against the wood, moans met by those of the aunt standing beside me and I was sure I was in hell.

The aunt sobbed, "My heart has betrayed me. It won't stop beating. Why will it not stop? It has betrayed me. Oh the deep pain. Now we will love him with such deep pain. Oh my Ivan, what was it that you couldn't tell us? What secret were you holding? If only you had told us. Everyone loved you. All your friends loved you, but you couldn't overcome yourself. Oh the psychological second. What was it that you couldn't tell us? Why won't my heart just stop? Why am I still here? I have lived 75 years, but my heart won't stop. What can I do? I can't rip in from my chest. Why won't it stop?"

The words came out of her, not with the speed of a waterfall pouring over a cliff. No, they were as slow as the drip of a faucet. Each drop was followed by silence; drip, silence, drip, silence. Each drip, though, was as strong as a wave, crashing against the rocks, but instead of rocks, it was the aunt being smashed. Relentless. Cruel. It was not the words, however, that pierced my heart, but the nothing in between.

It was in the nothing that her body took over, commandeering the brain with uncontrollable shaking and moaning. I will never forget the moaning that came from the depths of that shattered spirit. It was the groans that did me in. Pain washed over me with each one as I clutched her arm, trying to keep her from falling over.

I stood there silently, holding her arm, because what else could I do? He was gone and nobody knew why. There was an ugly truth hanging between us: Thirty-five is not the natural age at which to be buried. It is the time to live and love and find purpose. *Oh Ivan,* I thought. *Why did you pull the trigger? What happened in your mind that deciding second?*

The cross was bravely carried as the coffin followed it to a pre-dug hole. He was being laid to rest, but it didn't feel like it. Danny and I stood toward the back of the crowd, on either side of the aunt, holding her up. A friend of the deceased spoke a few words, but no priest came and no prayers were prayed: this final act of solace cruelly withheld from the family who needed it so desperately.

The church keeps its distance from such people. Its robes won't be tarnished by the damned. After the short speech, the coffin was lowered into the ground and the shovels were readied. As the first shovelful of dirt hit the wood of the coffin, the aunt's knees buckled. We squeezed her shaking arms tighter, afraid she would fall. Moans once again pressed me into a hell.

I thought my heart would break. I mean, physically explode. It was the same feeling as being held under water too long. A dull burning that spreads through the chest and ignites into fiery flames of pain as the mind calculates how many more seconds the lungs have. The heart screams its beats in warning. Death or life is seconds away and it doesn't matter which wins in that moment because either would seem like relief.

And then, it was all over. There was no more dirt to throw and I was still alive. My chest still burned, but I was breathing.

The candle was taken away and the lace which had been removed from the casket was folded up and put in a plastic grocery bag. Shovels scraped the dirt across the top of the closed hole, then the *bang bang* of the cross being pounded into the ground in place of a headstone gave way to an awful silence.

It was not the peaceful silence that comes with each morning as it welcomes a new beginning. It was the stagnant silence that I imagine hell to have. Like the feeling of being trapped under the sand in the middle of the great expanse of the desert, but being unable to die.

Danny and I came home completely depleted of words and emotions. The only thing that we could manage was to take the next breath. Even as I write this story, the ache in my chest returns. It is not as strong, but it is still there and I have learned to be okay with that.

The truth is, I never would have felt the pain that day with such force if I had not known what it is to be locked in the dark. I would not have stayed beside the aunt. Oh, my body would have, but my heart would have skipped on by leaving only an arm to hold. I had been locked in the dark though, and on that cold gray day, her darkness met mine and her waves of suffering crashed against mine. I stood next to her and even though we didn't share the same exact brand of pain, we didn't need to. It just hurt. It still does.

I didn't pretend to understand her pain, nor do I now. Her loss is completely, uniquely her own. And yet, her groanings so resembled the groanings of my heart. I knew what it was to hurt so bad that the air refused to re-enter my lungs. I too had been confused by the actions of others. The overwhelming force of the pain had also led me to cry out, "Why won't *my* heart just stop beating?" I knew, at least in part, why her heart was crying. I knew this because I had finally sat at the bottom of my lake. Sitting with her at the bottom of hers didn't feel so different.

POWER IN COMMUNITY

There is power in sharing, even if what is shared is pain. Community is not just a fool's belief, a grasping for wind. It's the promise of the Path Maker. He says that the path we walk on has been walked before, no matter what path it might be. There is a commonality in this journey we call life. And in the midst of pain and sadness, this truth holds power. Maybe not to turn the light on, but at least to reach out and find a friendly hand in the midst of the darkness.

There will be at least One with you in that locked room. I found that there were several. If you find only the One, retrace the paths of old. You will find many filled with pain and sadness. Lament is a theme, a major theme of the paths of the Path Maker. Those paths are there for a reason and they lead to exactly the same places as the paths of joy.

I had not realized this before because I never followed one of those paths to the end. Most times, I didn't even acknowledge those paths of pain. Honestly, even now, I feel unqualified to even write about sadness. I have a lot to learn on the matter, but if this story encourages some 'skippers' like me to slow down and fall to the bottom of the lake, to truly lament, then it is worth laying bare all that I'm learning.

I would love to say that all the sadness is gone, but that

would be a lie. Sometimes it comes crashing in like that wave and I go under, overwhelmed, gasping for air. Sometimes it comes from inside my own house and sometimes it is outside, but either way, the choice is mine. Will I thrash against it or will I let it wash over me?

Lamenting is about showing grief and sorrow and can even involve complaining. There must be room in our communities and in our hearts to express both grief and sorrow. Whole rooms just devoted to this. Maybe we are afraid that giving room to these thoughts will end in more darkness, a deeper despair, a free fall of the soul, but if we do it like the brave men and women in the Bible, it doesn't have to.

If we take the treasures from their paths to enrich our own, I believe it will not end that way. The Path Maker hasn't gone anywhere. He remains with us at the bottom of the lake and, down there, His goodness is tested and proven, once again, to be real and true. He is not changed by the brokenness and grief as we are: and that is why He becomes all the more precious to us.

He, once again, becomes all that we long for. He becomes the keeper of joy when we cannot hold it. He becomes the lover of our soul when we loathe our very souls. He becomes the resurrection and the life when we stare death in the face. In a fresh way, He becomes what He already is and what He has always been. He is not made uncomfortable by the depth of the water. He descended into hell, remember? And He will sit with us as long as it takes. His love endures forever and His patience is never exhausted.

He calls me to learn from Him even in this. This means that sometimes, in imitating Him, I am asked to keep joy, to love a soul and to cling to resurrection and life as I sit with someone under water. I am not the source of these things: joy, love, and resurrection and life. I am the skipping rock, remember? But because I have access to the source of all things through the Spirit, I receive full dispensing power.

I am an empty vessel and when filled by the Spirit, I am filled with those things. Incredible. In the power of the Spirit I can preserve joy in grief, love a soul in despair, and lean into the resurrection and life when death breathes down my neck. What a world I was missing when I refused to dip below the surface.

A deeper understanding of the power of the Spirit comes during these times as I pour out the goodness of the Path Maker on the soul at the bottom of the lake with me. Sometimes words are required in the dispensing process: a lot of times they are not. Any words deemed worthy of passing through the lips must be soaked in wisdom from above and prayed through. A process that, if practiced, would strain out what is unnecessary or harmful. Sometimes, we fill the silence with words when instead we should speak silent ones on our knees.

During my time under the surface, together with my one deepest human love, we had life-sustaining words spoken over us. Each of those words was said from hearts saturated in prayer for us, groaning in the spirit with us. They sat with us down there, at the bottom. And when the Spirit spoke, filling them up, they poured out only what He had said. Others sat down there and said nothing. They just sat and sat and sat. Both were vital and both agents of healing. The hasty plucked out what they thought of as encouragement, but was not. It damaged further.

WHO HURTS THE MOST?

These times are not to be weighed in a competition of who was and is in the most pain or whose pain feels the heaviest. A childhood friend of mine, who also tragically lost her dad, and I used to argue about who missed their dad the most. We loved comparing our pain. It was an endless competition of who hurt the most.

"Well I cried three times last week, I missed him so bad," She would start.

"That's nothing, I cried so hard that my eyes were still all red and puffy the next day," I countered.

"Yeah, well I kiss his picture each morning," Her retort was supposed to leave me ashamed at my lack of devotion.

"Yeah, well..."

This conversation might sound childish, but wait. Insert bigger words and more sophisticated sentence structure and you might cringe, realizing you have had this same conversation. Maybe we act this way because we want to validate the depth of our pain, which we assume can only be done if we minimize the hurt of others. To a hurting heart, this might make sense, but it's not a good excuse. There is never a good reason to tear another down, even if it is done because of deep pain. Pain hurts, no matter the depth, intensity, or duration and it is universal. We have all felt its force as it ripped through us.

I am realizing that I am not so unique in my pain. There are unique things about me that make me who I am, but pain is not one of them. What if the idea that no one can possibly understand my pain is a lie that seeks to isolate the wounded? I find comfort in the fact that my Path Maker and the mature people around me know or have known pain. It makes time spent at the bottom of the lake less lonely and a lot more useful because when the pain in one heart meets the pain in another, a moment of sacred fellowship is born: the intense fellowship of suffering. That is the kind of fellowship that I shared with both the aunt and then the mother at the graveside.

This fellowship does so much more than someone trying to twist a verse into grief like a light bulb is twisted into a socket. Life doesn't work that way. Coming alongside means slowing down and investing in someone else's pain and then agonizing with them in the Lord's presence. The fellowship of sorrow takes courage. That kind of entering in leaves you surrounded by their darkness and that is terrifying.

This darkness strips you down and leaves you naked, but when that nakedness is met with the sorrowful nakedness of another—a costly love is shared. A rare, costly love that is far too uncommon but, when unleashed, will change the world because it will change us.

This fellowship is not something new. It's just new to me. It's actually old and sacred. It started when Love stripped Himself of every glory and position and right and hung naked on the cross in order to meet my nakedness and match my pain. It hung in that horrible place as many looked on and ridiculed and made a way in the dark. It blazed a trail from hell all the way to heaven, giving me a way to follow. It cost everything: dignity, honor, and even life itself. But what it won was deemed worthy. Me. And you. Us. We are what was won.

Fellowship with us is what was secured. This is the Love that sits with you in your darkest, deepest despairs. And He has already made a way out. He will hold your hand as you emerge from those fathomless waters.

We do not stay at the bottom of the lake forever. It is not our home, thanks to Love Himself. It is a stop along the path, one "stop" He made as well. He stopped there before us and He will fill our lungs with enough air to make it back to the surface.

We are never alone. That truth gives us the stamina to feel the pain and sit in the sorrow bravely. Let's let the tears run down our cheeks unashamed. Each one is counted and kept by the Keeper of all. Love has explored the depths and conquered them. Fear is not mandatory anymore. And neither is skipping past.

Things Worth Remembering
- _Be ready to sit in the sadness as well as the joy_
- _Hasty advice and quick fixes damage further_
- _If you don't know what to say, great! Just sit_
- _Jesus sits with you_

September 16, 2020

Stop. Reflect. Push into to inconvenience of stillness & just be. Allow the thoughts to come to the surface, you know, the ones you've been pushing aside, burying under busyness. Allow the muscles to relax, listen to your body. Breathe. The pen can only move so fast; slow the racing mind down. Invite the Spirit into the mess of your soul. Listen.

It is one thing to enter into the pain and darkness of those around you, but it is quite another to be forced in and have the door locked behind you. The heart beats faster, pitch black in every direction.

My journal entry from that terrible day

A quiet village graveyard

Chapter 11:

SPILL OVER

A breath of life, a shift in sight
She's everything that's good.

Entering in can be a moment like it was at the graveside, sacred and spontaneous. I have not seen the aunt since that day, and I doubt that she would recognize me even if I did. What we shared was one intense hour. It was not the culmination of years of friendship. The choice to be present in each day, given as it is, will be filled with different kinds of entering in.

The isolated moments will be scattered throughout: a short conversation here, a listening ear there. These will not end in a long talk in a living room over a hot cup of coffee, which is just fine. Not every encounter will blossom to something greater; the ones that do usually grow slowly over time. It is never an explosion, but a slow deepening of trust. It's life shared that pushes the roots of friendship deeper and the leaves up higher toward the sun. It is not like growing lettuce, which shoots up and grows to maturity in the span of a month.

We are talking about tree-growing here: years of slow and steady. We planted a fig tree last year and this year harvested exactly one fig. It doesn't sound very impressive, but the older neighbors were intensely impressed that we even had one. Several years from now, we will have basketfuls. It will have been worth the wait, but it *will* take time.

Sitting at the kitchen table staring at the old wood stove, a fire burning inside, I knew it was lit just for me. It was lit with the last of the firewood for the winter even though it was supposed to be cold for another week at least. Experience had taught me that protest would be a waste of words because it was lit with all the love of a Simple Heart. That Simple Heart then served lunch. No meat, it was the end of the month, but if she had not apologized profusely for its absence, I wouldn't have even noticed. Roasted peppers stuffed with rice, salad, bread and homemade cake left little room on the table for meat. Oh, and coffee of course. There will always be room for coffee.

I was supposed to be working. I was supposed to be helping her plant seeds that were too little for her aged eyes to see and her weathered fingers to grasp. I was not, however, surprised, by the scene. She always made something when I came over, no matter the reason and no matter how long I stayed. It was not out of abundance, nor out of duty, although duty would require such a thing. It was love's fault.

We sat at the table to eat together, something I have learned over the past decade to anticipate. Sitting, sharing a meal. No rush. No agenda. Friends and food. She sat across from me, in between us her love offering; everything she had to give. I did not have to look in the cupboards or open the fridge to know it was the best food in the house. I knew her.

She always gave the best. We started eating and the rice melted in my mouth. It was cooked and seasoned perfectly. I asked in detail how she made it, knowing full well that my attempts would never compare, but wanting to try, to imitate her. She told me, step-by-step, explaining each detail with the assurance that it was not hard at all and that I could not go wrong.

"Now when you put it in the oven, just pour water in the pan, enough to cover the peppers half way. Even if you put a little less it will turn out just fine. See my pan there, on the stove? See that hole in the side of it? The water leaks out if I pour too much in. The peppers turned out just fine, so don't worry about the water. You are a great cook. They will turn out better than mine."

She then went on to tell the story of that mysterious hole. "I went outside to see what all the banging was and there he was attaching his jimmy-rigged satellite dish to the side of the house. I looked closer. The dish was my pan! He had snuck in the kitchen when I wasn't looking, taken the pan, drilled a hole in the side of it and attached to the side of the house. You better believe I took it back, right quick, but that hole gives me all kinds of trouble now. Everything leaks. Later today I need to scrub the stove. It's a mess."

I did not laugh. It would have been funny if she had been talking about her five-year-old son and not her seventy-five-year-old husband. Drilling a hole in a pan was one of his harmless shenanigans. Sometimes he is not so harmless, which I did not know for years, but the more I sit at that table, the more stories I hear. The more I enter into the love shown, be it lunch or coffee or a wool vest, the more that Simple Heart lets me enter into a life lived. And the more stories shared, the more obvious it becomes that her life has been hard. But somehow, the hardness has been softened by joy: just like rain softens the soil. And in this case, what has grown is a beautiful soul.

What I began to notice about each story, other than the hand of the Path Maker, was the tone of gratitude and delight in which it was told. Even the hard, dark stories shared this characteristic, which cannot be a coincidence. It is the pattern of her living and so her words follow right along. She is thankful for the difficult parts of her story as well as the good parts and, as a result, gratitude oozes out of her like the sweet fragrance of the first spring Peonies. Pure rapture: It entices you and fills your senses with wonder as you breathe in deeply.

THE GARDEN FAILURE THAT WASN'T A FAILURE

She did not receive a higher education, nor has she traveled more than a full-day's drive in any direction, but she lives in the never-ending world of delight. An attitude of gratitude has opened this up to her. She walks along, noticing every detail of her path, finding every treasure. She is not in a hurry and often stops just to take a deep breath and enjoy the fresh air.

Her ability to take life, without ignoring any part of it—all while being thankful for each piece of it—draws me into her world even more. It is something I long to emulate. And so, when she started talking about the dream to plant a garden, I was eager to walk down that road with her and spent time with her to learn her treasure-hunting skills. We talked and planned and agreed to give it a shot. We bought seeds, filled as many five-gallon water jugs as she had and the trunk would fit, and drove out to her husband's property in the village. It was the first trip of many, but each one held the same pattern.

We arrived, ate breakfast, because as she said with a grin, "how can you work without first filling your tank." Then we would take inventory of what supplies we brought and discuss what the priority was for that day. We worked for a couple of hours and then took a lunch break. Lunch was whatever we had made and brought, usually most of it being supplied by the Simple Heart. We ate and talked and listened to the birds. Then, we worked a little more before we headed home.

Other than a deeper appreciation for our farmers, I gained so much from that garden experiment. The garden part was a miserable failure. Lack of rain and time to commit to it resulted in an overgrown mess. Our onions, lettuce and peas were pristine, but as the season progressed and temperatures rose, so did the weeds and our harvest dwindled. We realized that age and lack of time were not on our side and that we had bitten off more than we could chew. The garden was too big for the two of us to manage, too far away, and too without water.

I had carefully set aside every Wednesday as my garden day, committing to one full day a week with some other afternoons thrown in. It was a great plan and very impractical. I forgot that I could not plan out nature's most important contribution to our garden: rain.

If it rained on Wednesday, we were unable to work the garden. It rained on several Wednesdays and we lost days of work, leaving us to play an impossible game of "Get that weed before it chokes out that carrot." The weed won more times than not, but even though it got most of our carrots, it could not choke out the delight of the Simple Heart. Every time we made our way out to that sad-looking garden, her eyes sparkled and her lips turned up in the purest of smiles.

I will always remember when the first peas were ready to harvest. She gently knelt down by the first plant and stroked the pod, tears filling her eyes.

"Oh, look how beautiful. Thank you, peas for giving us your fruit and thank you, Lord for making them grow. Look how big and plump they are. Oh look. Let's count this pod to see how many peas are inside. Twelve! Imagine that, twelve peas in just one pod. This one looks nice and long too, let's count it. Maybe it has more than twelve...so many beautiful peas. Look at them."

I did look and I too began to notice how beautiful not just the peas were, but also the plant that supported them. Such a fresh green with little curlicues here and there, waiting to grab onto whatever was nearby, climbing its way up toward the sun. Interspersed were the pods, hanging down like ornaments on a Christmas tree. We waited until they were nice and plump and then meticulously combed each plant pulling the full pods off the vine, careful not to disturb the ones still growing.

There was no way to rush anything in the garden, something which I found surprisingly irritating. I wanted to go and put in a full day of work and get "caught up," but my wise teacher knew better. This was not her first garden, and she kept reminding me that there was always work in a garden.

I wanted to have the satisfaction of finishing our job, but the weeds cared nothing for my desires. For me it became a never-ending unfinished project.

For my companion, I don't think the garden was a project at all. Maybe this was why she never seemed frustrated by the eternal to-do list it created. It was instead a living extension of our friendship. It was not something to get done, but something to be a part of together.

She would never take a break without me, never think to eat if I wasn't ready to eat as well, and always worked row-to-row next to me. It was all about delighting in each other and delighting in the growing of things. Yes, the weeds drove her crazy and I would often hear her say, "You are not wanted here" as she ripped out some crabgrass. She was sad, just as I was, that our experiment failed so terribly. But when we remember our days out working, it is always the conversations and songs that remain her focus and not the failure of the project. A focus of choice, I believe.

We choose what we focus on and what we emphasize in our memories. She chooses the things that bring delight. It is not a rejection of reality. Her life is not easy, nor has it ever been, but her habit of delighting gives her strength and wards off bitterness. Whether it is sitting at her table or working in a garden, her joy ignites mine and off we run together, continually, down the path of peas and stuffed peppers and pleasure in the presence of the Maker of all things grown.

PROFESSIONAL 'DELIGHTER'

The longer I work with her row-to-row and the more sitting I do with her at her table, I find her delights instructing mine. Pleasure pulls our hearts just like the current pulls the waves back out to sea. Solomon knew what happens when delight is misdirected. He misdirected it over 900 times and it pulled his heart to a place he had no intention of going. His warnings to a younger generation reveal the power of delight; it will form your heart in one way or another. Happiness—by that I mean true happiness, soul-satisfaction—is formed by delight in the things of the Lord. His Word, His people, His world, His Spirit, His Son, and He Himself are all promised sources of life-giving delight.

The Simple Heart, weeding next to me, knew that and lives that, which is why I will gladly stay in the next row waiting for her delight to spill over into me: forming my heart. I want to be pulled as far as she can pull me because I know that she will direct me right into the center of Delight itself. Her delights will become mine, at least in part, and mine will become hers.

This is the one of the greatest treasures along the paths of friendship we can take. Our delights are widened and deepened, enriched by the unique perspective of another. For all intents and purposes, we have nothing in common: not age, not country of origin, not social standing, and not interests (most at least). There is nothing that would lead to a natural bond and yet we are bound to each other. Years of drinking coffee with another can do that.

It has only been in the last year that all the coffee has given way to this level of delight-sharing. Each conscious decision to be present, to enter into the story of another doesn't require special skill, but it does imply a willingness to move closer and for that an openness to being seen. For just as I see more clearly up close, I am also, in the same way, seen more fully.

Everything is seen—the beautiful in me and the crooked— which is why it is such a privilege to sit at tables and eat meals like the one I ate that day with the Simple Heart. It becomes even more than the sharing of a story and an exchange of delights. It becomes being seen without fear and without shame. That is what true friendship is about: We crave it and when we find it, joy springs up within us.

Joy mined from the right source both gives strength and

opens up a new world once hidden within our own. It is what allows so much thankfulness to flood into the life of the Simple Heart. She lives each day enjoying, at the very least, the One who made her and then all His gifts to her, even if it is a simple pea pod. When you find an expert delighter like her, get ready for some treasure hunting. And by all means stay in the next row, close enough to lap up the delight that spills over.

Things Worth Remembering

- *Be patient when building relationships*
- *Find and spend time with an expert 'delighter'*
- *Freely delight in good things*
- *Let others see and participate*

Our garden before the weeds took over

My friend, The Simple Heart, and I shelling peas

Chapter 12:

I REALLY AM NAKED

And more than that, the wood's transformed
And my fear has melted away.

Gardens are planted in rows. And sometimes in life, we, like the plants I'm learning to grow, want to pretend that focusing on our own row will keep distractions or interruptions to a minimum. Keeping yourself in the next row over is a decision of the will most of the time. But it isn't a safe distance. Everything happening in one row will affect the other. Weeds missed in one will grow up to cast shade on and to crowd out good plants growing in the row beside. Weeds flung carelessly could crush the tender seedlings sprouting up in the other. They are completely connected from one end to the other— even if the things growing in them are as different as watermelon and corn, proximity connects them. A true garden is made up of many rows. One row of watermelons is not an impressive garden, but get ten or twenty different things growing and the color and variety is dazzling. How each one grows, looks, and tastes is science, but the combining of their flavors and colors requires skill. The possibilities end only when the creativity of the chef runs out. But sometimes possibilities are thwarted before the chef even gets into the kitchen when an unwanted intruder sneaks in and destroys the garden before the harvest.

GARDEN INTRUDERS

"They just come in and eat all the vegetables. I don't know what I'm going to do. They trample everything and take whatever they want. The Black people are completely ruining the garden."

I looked up from my plate of deliciousness, most of it from that aforementioned garden, and looked over at Danny. He was nodding his head, as his fork lifted another bite towards his open mouth. It was open to receive food, mine was just open. I tried to stay engaged, "How do they get into the garden?" I asked and sincerely wanted to know.

"They just come in from the woods. See how the garden is just at the edge of those trees? That is a large wood and they come right in," replied my host.

"Well, what are they doing in the woods?" I pressed. I could see out of the corner of my eye that Danny was looking at me. *He must be so proud that I am interacting so well and asking questions,* I thought.

"The black people live there," continued the host.

"Live there? What do you mean? They live right there in the woods?"

"Ummm, yeah. Lots of them."

"Why do they come into the garden?"

"They must be hungry. I am going to have to build a fence to keep them out."

"Do you think a fence will work?" I wasn't trying to be rude, but I could climb most fences by the time I was eight. It did not seem like a rock-solid plan.

"Oh sure, they can't jump high fences."

Danny nodded his head in agreement. I blinked really fast several times, but not even that helped me make sense of the story. Afraid of seeming impolite by questioning the logic of our generous host's fence plan, I dropped it and dove back into my dinner, fork first.

"You were really into that story at dinner," Danny commented later.

"Well yeah, can you believe that Black people live in the

woods and sneak in to eat his vegetables? It is the craziest thing I have ever heard. Plus, I haven't even seen any Black people here."

"Oh Wendy," Danny said before laughing hysterically. "Do you know what the word *srna* means?"

"No...," I clearly didn't get what was so funny.

"It wasn't *Black people* in the garden, it was *deer*. He was saying *srna*, deer, not Black people."

Now I was laughing. "That makes so much more sense. Seriously though, why are those words so similar? Is this language trying to torture me?"

"Maybe." He grinned, his eyes dancing.

The woods, the deer, the irresistible veggies and even the fence made sense. Obviously, our friend would build a fence. And obviously deer would not be able to climb it with their fingerless hooves. It was the most logical solution to his problem. Deer, the destructive intruders, needed clear boundaries as our friend and his family relied on their garden for food. He was a vigilant gardener, who knew exactly what he was doing, unlike his clueless dinner guest.

WHEN IT STOPS BEING FUNNY

Being clueless was not a part of my personality—at least not until I was in a free-fall of adventure, interacting on a daily basis with others in a second language. But 'black deer' has become an inside joke between Danny and I. There is something healthy and freeing about being able to laugh at yourself and move on. Metaphorically face-planting in Serbian gave me plenty of occasions for just that.

Most times, I would laugh off my blunders and move on, pushing ahead to my goal, a place where the sign read "fluent," which would be my exit out of Cluelessville. But, when those blunders came every day, multiple times a day, they started to rub. It's all a part of the process, but when that process is your life, you start to feel like the shredded garden where those sneaky deer have been wreaking havoc and tearing everything apart—one mouthful at a time. This venture through the unknown was obliterating me.

Well, at least it felt that way on many levels. Everything in me was shouting, *this is too hard. It's just too different. It doesn't make sense. It never will.* The thought rampage began, and soon the physical tears would follow. I have been there many times, sometimes several times a day. Committing to understand something, be it a language, or a culture, or a person who is completely different from you, will send you down the same hole and like Alice in Wonderland, you will find yourself in a different world.

My reaction—more accurately, my defense mechanism—is to build something around me. I nicely fence off the garden row that is me—to protect myself from the intruding deer, which is whatever I am facing that is different.

I can grow and thrive, I tell myself, pest-free. I can even add some barbed wire just in case those deer grow fingers and start climbing my fence. Better yet, I'll make it a wall, better safe than sorry.

There I sit, one sad, lonely walled-off garden row, cowering at the slightest sound from the woods. I can grow like that and fill out my row if the conditions are right. A little sun, a little rain, some weeding and I look good. Come harvest time I will be ready. There is just one problem. That isn't enough for me anymore. I have had enough of being a single row. I want the whole garden! But for that, my walls must come down: each one of them. Isn't that what all of these stories have been? The falling of crooked walls? With each crash, I feel just a little more exposed until I am back in that reoccurring dream, completely naked. But that is only half the story. It is real, raw and painful, but it is only half.

WATERMELON SALAD: THE OTHER HALF

The crooked made straight, the depths discovered and the treasures found exist in the other half, but to get there, I first had to walk the first half. I had to de-wall my row; I had to immerse myself in the whole garden. Every story that you have read took place in a foreign setting and would have been missed if I had stayed in my row with my barbed-wired walls. No walls means opening myself up to whatever is out there and yes, deer might come in for a snack, but the wonders and tastes of the garden keep me coming back for more.

I have come to long for the whole garden and not just a monochromatic row. I am learning to love all the colors, shapes and flavors mixed together. I love watermelon. It is the taste of summer: refreshing and sweet. When I start to see those green orbs at the Farmers Market, I know we will be eating watermelon every day until there are none left to buy. As far as I am concerned, the garden could be made of only the watermelon row. I had lived happily in my green and pink world until a chef friend of ours ruined it all.

This chef friend came to our city in order to host a live

cooking show at our church. Once a week, for six weeks, he cooked up some concoction of splendor for the audience to try. As he cooked and talked, we learned to make these recipes along with cooking shortcuts and new techniques. One week, I saw watermelon on the counter next to him as he set up his cooking station: I knew it was going to be a good night.

He welcomed us and started off by cooking up the main dish. I have no idea what it was. I was looking at the watermelon. Then he turned to the watermelon and instead of putting it on the plate next to the main dish like a normal person, he began to desecrate it. He had already cut off the rind and cut it into cubes, but then he started adding different things to the bowl. First, he chopped up a generous amount of mint and threw it in. Not such a shocking combination. I was still excited to try it. Then he cut up some red onion. In it went. Feta cheese was next–that is when I started to question his credentials. When he pulled out a tomato, I tried to remain calm. As he mixed everything together with complete confidence, I was bracing myself for the first taste of this weird salad.

As I stared in disbelief, I was 100% sure that it would be disgusting. When he offered me that salad, the only thing that made me put some on my plate was my curiosity. I sat down in my seat and raised my fork to my mouth. It was perfection. Somehow, all of the flavors mixed together in exactly the right way. They balanced each other out. Each ingredient pulled the best flavor out of the other ingredients. They blended so well that it was difficult to tell where one flavor started and the other ended. I was shocked. I never would have put those ingredients together: nor did I think they would work together.

The chef knew better. Not only had he created something new and exciting for me, but also something surprising. I actually think that I enjoyed eating that watermelon salad even more than eating watermelon by itself. In a tiny way, he had expanded my known world by pushing me into the unknown world of watermelon salad. It was more than a new experience. It changed the way that I thought about different flavors and the potential they had to work together.

It was just a salad, but it shifted my perspective. It triggered my brain to start thinking about combinations in general, not just in the kitchen. What else was I missing out on because I thought it was weird? What other flavors from the garden could be combined in ways I hadn't thought possible? Suddenly I loved the whole garden a little more and wanted to explore all that it had to offer. One little taste of watermelon salad did all that. My love of watermelon was deepened and expanded into love of all that could be combined with and put alongside it. I realized for the first time that pairing it with something very different than itself like a tomato, for example, actually enriched its own flavor. And that's when I also had the realization that changed the way I thought about everything.

WHAT WE GET IN RETURN

It may sound silly to compare myself to food, but these stories are my journey toward becoming watermelon salad. Some parts of me were the rind being cut off. Some moments were filled with pain as I went from whole to cubed. Others parts of my story were like adding mint and onion, logical choices. Still others were the wild cards: life's tomatoes and feta cheese. But I hope you have seen how each has worked together with the existing ingredients to enrich me and to bring out my full flavor.

Color has been added as well as flavor. With all of the ingredients mixed together, the meal is ready to be served. And just like the chef was attempting to expand my palate, this book has been my attempt to expand your perception of the unknown.

Hard is only half the story, an important and necessary half, but incomplete without the other. Moving through the first half has brought me to the joys of the second half. This is not to say that I am done with the unknown. It's all around me and, in ways, I am starting the journey all over again each time I enter into something new. The unknown of these stories, however, has become known and I have moved into the other half. Moving closer and not further away. Giving myself and receiving another: seeing what is really there. In the other and by the other has led me to a new kind of seeing and being. It has opened me up to love all that I see and to hold it with honor and respect. That kind of seeing will transform the heart—and a heart transformed is a life enriched. Of course, like with many wonderful pursuits of life, there is a catch.

This type of seeing cannot be from a distance. I must dig into and immerse myself in it. Then, over time, I will grow from noticing to seeing and then from seeing to loving. Maybe not accepting of or agreeing with everything, but loving that which is different. As least, that has been my story. Love gives me freedom to move in closer and open myself up to see the part of others I wish I had never seen and to show the part of myself that I used to wish I didn't have. I am learning what it means to have authentic relationships: to explore the depths.

It is because of this that 'different,' as a concept, has lost the title of the intruder in my life. It has not destroyed my life as I feared it might. Change was crucial and inevitable. Just like the watermelon had to be prepared for the salad, I also had to face transformation. Things were cut off, shapes were changed but as a whole, the watermelon was not ruined.

Those changes were made with purpose and so were the changes wrought in me. It was His way of pulling out my full and unique flavor as He paired me with different. Each thing that was stripped away or reshaped was preparation. I remain Wendy, but without some of the junk and now I am ready to be thrown in the bowl with whatever different or unknown thing that awaits me. I can say that bravely, not because I think it will be easy; it will not. My bravery comes from knowing the Chef.

He is also the Builder, still holding the plumb line in his strong yet gentle hand. He has been rebuilding and continues to slowly rebuild my heart. I was in many ways torn down to the bare foundation of who I am, but with a very specific plan: to get rid of those crooked walls. This prep work was essential for the next step, which was rebuilding. As the plumb line was dropped over and over again, so was the unstable removed: the teetering walls were knocked over to make room for straight ones. Being on the other side of the rebuild has given me perspective into the purpose of the hard process. It was not hard because the Builder was being cruel or destructive. It was hard because it was a complete reconstruction of me. Anyone who has renovated a house knows that the process is time-consuming, costly, and messy, but the outcome makes all the sweat and tears worth it. If the process is allowed to continue until completion, the new and improved is so much better than the original. That is why I live with anticipation knowing both what the unknown offers me and knowing the One who will walk beside me through it. I am confident of this because He has used the unknown to recreate me and He has in the process shown His unwavering faithfulness. Never has He tried to trick or take advantage of me. He has always stayed right beside me: to realign and rebuild.

This process continues today and I am learning to lean into it and not to resist it. I admit that there is still a lot of work to do, but have seen enough of the renovation to get the vision of the Builder. All of the changes He makes in me are in order to better me and I trust Him in a new and deeper way because of all that we have been through together. As He takes on new projects in my heart, I know that He is working to free me of the crooked so that I can live life to the fullest in all of its pain and delights.

This type of life is not only for me. The same thing is offered to you. Different isn't going anywhere. It's all around you. Will you enter in and start the process of recreation? A journey of that breadth will take time. It will change you and change often hurts. You might lose yourself for a while along the way, but I am here, sharing with you that it is worth it.

I would not trade my life for any other. I would not live in any other place. I'm not a super human or super spiritual, nor do I need to be. I just need to be willing: willing to walk into the unknown with my Path Maker and Guide. Without Him, I would have never made it. I would not have even had the courage to take the first step.

Entering into a different world is always scary, uncharted territory, but the Path Maker promises to accompany us as we go. He is our Guide with complete knowledge of the trail. He will lead us through valleys and up to mountaintops but no matter the terrain, He never gets lost. And so, if we are careful to stay beside Him, neither will we. As we go, we will realize that just as much as the prepared path is His gift to us, even more so is His presence with us. I hope this shifts our perspective enough to say, "Yes, I want to enter into the journey. I will trust You. I will walk with You wherever the path leads."

What awaits is the adventure of a lifetime: the rebuilding of a heart.

Our chef friend hosting his live cooking show in our city

Watermelon salad anyone?

DISCUSSION QUESTIONS

Chapter 1: Exposed

1. How would you feel if you found yourself in the 'naked dream'?
2. Describe an experience that left you feeling exposed.
3. In what ways did you resist the feeling?
4. How did you eventually move past those feeling into ones of acceptance?
5. Think about a time when you left something or someone familiar for you? What were you feeling?

Verse for meditation:

"The thief comes only to steal and kill and destroy; I came so that they would have life, and have it abundantly."

–John 10:10 NASB

Chapter 2: No-Man's-Land

1. What did the initial steps of entering the unknown look like for you?
2. Describe the moments you were overwhelmed.
3. What were the contributing factors?
4. Was/Were there any moment(s) of peace amidst the chaos? What was it that brought peace?
5. In what ways did you feel God's presence with you?
6. What are some things that you had to relearn?
7. In what ways did that process leave you feeling lost?

Verse for Meditation:

"Do not fear, for I am with you;
Do not be afraid, for I am your God.
I will strengthen you, I will also help you,
I will also uphold you with My righteous right hand."

–Isaiah 41:10 NASB

Chapter 3: Special Needs and the Language Brain

1. In what areas has the plumb line been dropped in your life? Retell the entire story.
2. What was found to be crooked?
3. How was it found to be crooked? What did the process of rebuilding look like?
4. What toll did learning something new take on your body? Mind?
5. How was your trust in the Builder deepened through the process?

Verse for meditation:

"See, I have appointed you this day over the nations and over the kingdoms,
To root out and to tear down,
To destroy and to overthrow,
To build and to plant."

–Jeremiah 1:10 NASB

Chapter 4: Missing What is Right There

1. What are the distractions in your life?
2. What does the pace of your life say about your priorities?
3. Why is it so difficult to live life at Jesus' pace?
4. What helps you to slow down?
5. What have you seen when you slowed down that you were missing before?
6. How did the Voice guide you through the process?

Verse for meditation:

"Take My yoke upon you and learn from Me, for I am gentle and humble in heart, and you will find rest for your souls."

–Matthew 11:29 NASB

Chapter 5: Cockroaches and Pressed Slacks

1. How would you define hope?
2. How have your life experiences challenged that definition?
3. How has your hope been challenged by the experiences of those around you?
4. How have those challenges, from your experience and others, reshaped your relationship with hope?
5. How does all of this tie into Jesus being your hope?

Verse for meditation:

"But as for me, I will be on the watch for the Lord;
I will wait for the God of my salvation.
My God will hear me."

−Micah 7:7 NASB

Chapter 6: Entering to Exit

1. How have you found honesty to be vital in your relationships?
2. Why do we sometimes avoid being honest with each other?
3. How can bravely and graciously addressing dishonesty impact our relationships?
4. In what ways have you see God use a part of you that you thought was useless?
5. What has He restored in you?
6. How has that influenced your relationship to Him?

Verse for meditation:

"Better is open rebuke
Than love that is concealed."

–Proverbs 27:5 NASB

Chapter 7: A Poem by the Sea

1. Retell the story of a time that you misjudged a person or situation because you assumed something that turned out to be untrue.
2. How did you discover the truth?
3. What did it feel like when you learned the truth?
4. What happened after you learned the truth?
5. How do you stop yourself from assuming and making the same mistake again?

Verse for meditation:

"Listen to advice and accept discipline,
So that you may be wise the rest of your days."

–Proverbs 19:20 NASB

Chapter 8: Cigarette Butts in the Maternity Ward

1. What has uncharted territory looked like in your life?
2. In what ways was the unknown scary and/or hard?
3. In what ways was it an exciting adventure?
4. What treasures did you find along the way?
5. What did you learn about the Path Maker?
6. How has the way you face new unknown territory changed because of this experience?

Verse for meditation:

"And the Lord is the one who is going ahead of you; He will be with you. He will not desert you or abandon you. Do not fear and do not be dismayed."

–Deuteronomy 31:8 NASB

Chapter 9: Scribbles

1. Describe a time that your motives have gone from great to selfish?
2. How did you realize that they had changed?
3. What did the process of getting them 'back on track' look like for you?
4. How does God correcting our warped motives reveal His love for us and His grace toward us?
5. How does that impact the way that you relate to Him?

Verse for meditation:

"Therefore let's approach the throne of grace with confidence, so that we may receive mercy and find grace for help at the time of our need."

–Hebrews 4:16 NASB

Chapter 10: One Skip Short

1. How do you respond to sadness: sadness in your own life and in the life of those around you?
2. In what ways does it seem better to skip right by all sadness?
3. What are the benefits of feeling sadness to its full extent?
4. How have you been met and helped in your sadness by others and by God?
5. How have these difficult, sad experiences shaped the person you are today?
6. How is comparing pain damaging?

Verse for meditation:

"Do not rejoice over me [amid my tragedies], O my enemy!
Though I fall, I will rise;
Though I sit in the darkness [of distress], the Lord is a light for me."

Micah 7:8 AMP

Chapter: 11 Spill Over

1. How are some relationships more like trees than lettuce?
2. How do you 'share life' with others?
3. Think of a person who has greatly influenced you over a period of many years. What is it about them that impacted you? Why was that so impactful?
4. What did you learn from the experience?

Verse for meditation:

"Oil and perfume make the heart glad,
And a person's advice is sweet to his friend."

–Proverbs 27:9 NASB

Chapter 12: I Really *Am* Naked

1. What is the unknown for you right now?
2. Where are you in the process (the hallway, excited, overwhelmed and dazed, being corrected and redirected, sitting at the bottom of the lake, at the other side looking back)?
3. Explain what the process has looked like for you so far?
4. What fears do you still have?
5. What good have you seen come from your bravery to enter the unknown?
6. How does knowing that hard is only half of the story change your perspective of the unknown?

Verse for meditation:

"Have I not commanded you? Be strong and courageous! Do not be terrified nor dismayed, for the Lord your God is with you wherever you go."

–Joshua 1:9 NASB

ACKNOWLEDGEMENTS

Where to begin? It would be impossible to thank each person who has been a part of the living and the writing of this book. This is an incomplete list, but each person mentioned has played a special role in this particular project.

Danny, "thank you" doesn't even come close to conveying my gratitude for the support and constant encouragement you have been to me. Your prompting was the reason I started writing this book at all, your willingness to rearrange your schedule the reason I had the time and space to write it, and your initial feedback to the first rough draft the reason I kept revising until it was right. You have faithfully stood next to me throughout the process of this entire project; a priceless gift. I love you.

Kristin, your gift for editing and coaching new writers was essential for, not only the completion of this book, but also the growth in me as an author. Your friendship throughout the process made the editing phase much more bearable. Thank you for selflessly pouring into me.

Thank you Maria for your sharp eye and mind in editing the manuscript.

Thank you mom, even though you were geographically far away from me when I was writing, our phone conversations provided encouragement that pushed me along. Also, thank you for clearing space in your garage to store my books.

Thank you Tadija for being you. You have opened my eyes and shifted my perspective many times as you tirelessly seek answers to your questions. This has undoubtedly not only influenced me as a person, but also as a writer. Thank you for opening up new wonders to me every day as you soak in the world around you. I love you, my Jumping Bean.

Thank you to each person who is mentioned in these written stories. Thank you for opening your hearts to me and accepting mine in friendship.

Thank you to everyone who read the manuscript and gave feedback. You were a vital part of the process.

Thank you Novi Život Kragujevac. You are not just a place to go on Sundays, but a family that I belong to. Thank you for listening to my endless updates and babblings about this book and supporting me through each phase by your prayers and friendship. Watching you step out to discover the gifts God has given you has inspired me to step into and discover mine.

ABOUT THE AUTHOR

Wendy Zahorjanski is a nonfiction writer whose life has been an incredible journey guided by faith. After originally coming from a small-town, she heeded the divine call that led her to traverse continents and cultures. Venturing down unfamiliar paths in foreign lands, Wendy's life has been an extraordinary adventure—a blend of laughter, tears, resilience, and moments of doubt. Through the lens of her own experiences—relocating to a foreign land, learning a new language, embracing motherhood, forging connections, navigating through pain's shadows, and much more—Wendy's writing goal is to unveil the amazing moments of opportunity and spiritual growth concealed within seemingly insurmountable moments. She resides in Kragujevac, Serbia with her husband, son, and large boxer named Sven.

ABOUT THE ILLUSTRATOR

Mirjam Klop is an artist, mother of two, member care specialist, wife, and full-time cross-cultural worker. She is from Leiden, Holland, but has called many cities and countries home. At the age of 18 she felt the Lord calling her to join Youth with a Mission in Amsterdam. For the past 30 years she has been living out that call in Hungary, Romania, and Serbia, where she and her family reside today. When she is not leading art workshops or training young people on effective cross-cultural communication, she enjoys cooking, drinking coffee with friends and of course drawing.

Made in the USA
Middletown, DE
30 October 2023